CORRIDOR OF TIME IN KENYA

THROUGH MAU MAU DAYS
&
INDEPENDENCE YEARS

LOUISE ELLIS

ISBN 1 85863 017 7

First Published 1993 by
MINERVA PRESS
1 Cromwell Place
London SW7 2JE

Second Impression 1994
Third Impression 1995

Printed in Great Britain
B.W.D. Ltd., Northolt, Middlesex

CORRIDOR OF TIME IN KENYA

THROUGH MAU MAU DAYS
&
INDEPENDENCE YEARS

LOUISE ELLIS

CONTENTS

ILLUSTRATIONS

A SKETCH

The Old Sub Chief.

ASSORTED BLACK AND WHITE PHOTOGRAPHS

The Author

Cheetah

Zebra in Game Park.

Lions in Nairobi Game Park.

Maureen with 'Charlie the Chimp'.

Valerie and Elaine with a new playmate.

Peter with Valerie and Elaine in later years.

A Masai warrior.

Masai herd boys on the Ngong Hills.

Valerie and Elaine make friends on Safari with a Masai mother and children.

A farewell to Local Government.

Val's farewell walk at Anmer House prior to leaving for Australia.

INVITATIONS

An invitation to the Inauguration Garden Party for the Republic of Kenya.

FOREWORD

I commend this book to all those who have lived in East Africa because its vivid descriptions of the scenery and wildlife will stir nostalgic memories. To those who have not been lucky enough to have had that experience, I commend to them the story of the author's incredible courage in facing a series of almost unbelievable disasters, and yet keeping a high morale mixed with an impish sense of humour.

In spite of the continued post war attacks by the media on Colonialism and its reputed repression, the author has given lie to their view that the white man was unable to have an excellent rapport and friendship with Africans, in her case from servants to Cabinet Ministers. The press said that we were paternal, as though that was a sin. Western Europe could benefit now from the kind of happy family which the book portrays and the human man who was their *pater familias*. What the African did not have was political freedom and the same writers during the last twenty five years have been remarkably silent about the results of gaining that freedom, except to record the miseries of internecine warfare.

The author talks of "Africa the stealer of hearts that never lets one go. It casts a magic indefinable spell". We felt that we gave our best years to that country. That magic spell was our reward.

SIR WALTER COUTTS, GCMG, MBE

Last Governor-General of Uganda.
(Now deceased)

For my family and all my good friends with whom I have shared happiness enjoyed but of a few.

CHAPTER ONE

ON LEAVING AND ARRIVING

It was our last Saturday in Kenya.

"Memsahib, Kiambu is crying because you are leaving."

The old sub-chief stood on our verandah, hugging his battered army hat, his cheap plastic raincoat dripping pools of precious Kenya rain on the floor around him, his wise old eyes showing concern for our sadness at leaving our home of twenty years. He had been our friend, helping us in many ways, and had now come to collect a few things we wished him to have.

His words came back as we leaned out of the train window as it slowly moved out of Nairobi station to take us down to the port of Mombasa. Our dear friends of many years, a forlorn group on the platform, waiting their turn to leave this beautiful land, sadly waved us good-bye. Our family doctor had raced through the barrier and chased the train shouting,

"I had no idea you were going so soon. Good luck and God bless you."

The French have a saying that when you leave a person a part of you dies. It almost seemed that now we were leaving Kenya, all of me was dying. Indeed a kaleidoscope of memories of this twenty year corridor of time flashed through my mind comparable with the claim that people who narrowly miss death see their whole lives flash before them. Memories of joy, gaiety, sadness, struggle and danger, but above all, a love affair with a country that would last for ever.

I turned to see my daughters, now in their twenties, struggling to control their tears. I remembered another station in England where three small children and myself were boarding another train and waving good-bye to friends and weeping grandparents. We were on our way to be united with my husband who had been in Kenya for three months and who had now sent for us to join him. I was feeling guilty that I could not feel too much unhappiness or concern for the people we were leaving behind as I was so excited about the journey ahead and the anticipated joy of seeing my husband again. The children too had caught this air of excitement and I hoped did not seem too casual with their farewells. Anxious relatives and others had warned us of the danger of taking small children into a country where Mau Mau was rife, as these were the days when Jomo Kenyatta was being hounded by the British Security Forces prior to his imprisonment. I tried to placate them by saying my husband would not have allowed us to travel unless he thought we would be safe and that our place was with him. But I did feel for the grandparents and cheered them by saying we would write very regularly and that we would be returning to see them on our leaves.

We had never flown before and in those days the trip from London to Kenya took three days by Viking aircraft. What an adventure it seemed to me! Comparing it with today's non-stop jet flights it seems all the pleasure of travel has gone and I would turn the clock back any time to that first journey by air. Lunch in Nice sitting by the blue Mediterranean; a night stop in Malta at the Phoenicia Hotel with time to digest the luxuries of the hotel, the harbour lights at night, the monks, the tolling of the bells, the donkeys and the architectural differences. Up next morning at 5am and over the sea to North Africa with a stop on the desert for refuelling; our first contact with Arabs and flies and sticky orange juice drinks and the shock that we as Britishers were not all that welcome. Then on to Khartoum for our second night stop at the Grand Hotel where we found the staff on strike and we had to help ourselves to drinks. Someone eventually served us with potato soup and fried sardines which in the heat of June was hardly welcome fare, but it didn't seem to matter. We consoled ourselves with John Collins drinks sitting on the banks of the Nile and when a frog sat near my chair I was not all that confident he was real! On again at 5am to Juba on the borders of Sudan and Uganda, relishing the views and the strange sight of coal black Sudanese officers at the banda type airport buildings, flashing their eyes and snow white teeth. These buildings had thatched roofs supported by wooden posts. A low wall at the base allowed air to flow through this open space, from roof to wall, which was very much appreciated in a hot climate. We were driven to a small hotel for lunch which was surrounded by frangipani, bougainvillaea and hibiscus and now we began to sense the real African atmosphere. By mid afternoon on the third day we were landing at Entebbe airport in Uganda and it almost seemed as if we were going to land in Lake Victoria instead of on its shores as the runway is so close to the water. When we entered the airport buildings, little did we dream of the historical events which would take place there in the years to come. It was a sleepy little place with swarms of flies and mosquitoes; hot, humid and tropical.

As we took off on the last leg to Nairobi, the heavens decided to give us a memento of our trip as we flew through five storms over Uganda and the great Rift Valley and landed in Nairobi on one engine! But there to make it all worthwhile was the one we had come all this way to be with, my dear husband, beaming with delight at the sight of his beloved family.

This all happened a long time ago. It is 20 years since we sailed out of Mombasa harbour on our way to Australia, but the memories are still with us, for Kenya is a most inspiring land. Recently, as I stepped over my allotted span of years, I had a great desire to tell my story of how it was then. The turmoil in Africa goes on. Who knows the answer to its problems and if they ever will be resolved. Sir Walter Coutts (now deceased) was a Cabinet Minister in Kenya for many years and also Governor General in Uganda for two years at the end of his career. He prepared a foreword for this book before he died. I quote a little from this foreword:

"In spite of the continual attacks by the media on Colonialism and its reputed repression, the author gives the lie to their views that the White man was unable to have an excellent rapport and friendship with Africans, in her case from Cabinet Ministers to servants. The Press said that we were paternal as though that was a sin. What the African did not have was political freedom, but the same Press during the last 30 years has been remarkably silent about the results of gaining that freedom, except to record the miseries of internecine warfare."

"The author talks of Africa the stealer of hearts that never lets one go. It casts a magic indefinable spell. We felt that we gave the best years of our lives to that country. That magic spell was our reward."

I add a thought that there have always been floods and droughts in Africa, but in Kenya the colonialists catered for these by their tremendous agricultural efforts, thus avoiding the dreadful famines of the present time. They can be acclaimed for preventing the horrific suffering and the deaths of thousands of adults and children from starvation. In times of flood, food and supplies were dropped by aircraft to remote villages and district officers always took care of their welfare.

I look back and remember my loved one who died there in 1965 and all my good friends. The majority of colonialists of that time all left and scattered themselves throughout many countries in the world, and I know they left a part of themselves there. Their distant footsteps still echo down the corridors of time in that land beside the Indian Ocean.

CHAPTER TWO

EARLIER YEARS

As a young girl growing up in England, I never dreamed that one day I would go to Africa, but I did go and my life was never the same again. All the pent up memories of that time are the story of this book. It is part of the African scene, Africa the great enigma, Africa the stealer of hearts that never lets one go. It casts a magical, indefinable spell.

I grew up in North Yorkshire at my grandfather's estate, Blansby Park. It was situated in beautiful wide open spaces; areas of moors, dales and woodlands with rippling streams and I loved the country life. My father died from wounds he received in the first world war so my mother, brother and I lived there with grandparents, aunts, uncles and cousins. We were a close and happy family. It was a large estate with a dairy herd, cattle, sheep, pigs, poultry, mixed crops and orchards. We kept staff and a gamekeeper who reared pheasants, partridges and guinea fowl in preparation for the shooting parties which arrived in September each year.

The days were hard and long before the advent of tractors and milking machines. Our Clydesdale horses were invaluable and great care was taken of their welfare. I had a pony called Peggy, the delight of my young life, and I escaped with her many, many times to ride across the beautiful countryside in the bracing, refreshing air of early mornings or evenings.

The seasons passed along with their various chores, ploughing, sowing and reaping and the days started at 6am and ended at nightfall, whatever the season. In Springtime our woodlands were a picture with their carpets of primroses, violets, bluebells, anemones and columbines. The birds considered the same woodlands their paradise; squirrels, rabbits and hares abounded. The streams were full of trout where the men folk relaxed, quietly fishing and reflecting, whenever possible. In Spring too, the baby lambs came along and we often had several orphans to care for. One of my uncles trained gun dogs and sheep dogs. His kindness, care and infinite patience when he worked with them was unbelievable.

Summer days were long. During the school holidays we often had to help with fastening the hens up in their houses at night. How tedious it was at 11pm to find the last stragglers refusing to go inside. We would chase them, curse them until they finally surrendered. In hay time and harvest we would help to take the "drinkings" out to the men in the fields. These would be huge baskets of meat pies, fruit pies and scones full of lovely farm butter, also large cans of tea or gale beer if it was a hot day. Gale is a herb which grows in Yorkshire from which this delicious brew is made. The men knew that we longed to partake in this feast and they always left sufficient for us, after a little teasing!

Autumn was a dreamy time. All the leaves in the woodlands were a mass of gold, red and brown. The sunsets were hazily beautiful. The fields were ploughed to lay fallow until planting time in Spring. The yearly agricultural fairs were held in the market towns when the farm-hands could either leave and find a new employer or be taken on again for a further year by their present one. Most of ours stayed until retiring age.

In winter we would often be snowed in for as long as 3 to 4 weeks at a time and how happy we were not to have to go to school. We would feel snug and warm in the big kitchen on baking days as we watched the bread, teacakes, scones, cakes, pies and other goodies being prepared. Huge amounts of these were required for such a large household. Sometimes we would be sent to the attics to check the stored apples. These were individually wrapped in tissue paper and had been laid in neat rows on the attic floors. We had to remove the suspected bad ones. Above our heads rows of hams and sides of bacon hung from the rafters.

It was a wonderful, magic life seen through the eyes of a child but, of course, as I grew older my grandfather demanded a sense of responsibility from me as he did from all his grandchildren. We had to learn to groom a horse, milk a cow, feed calves, feed poultry, collect eggs and check the incubators which incessantly spewed out hundreds of little chicks. He taught us all about flowers, vegetables and fruit trees and gave us all a small garden of our very own so that we could watch our own flowers, vegetables and soft fruits grow. He was a wonderful man and my grandmother was a true lady who loved us all.

Growing up naturally brought changes. Sadly my grandparents died, my mother remarried and the second world war reared its ugly head. My brother went off with a cousin to serve in the Royal Navy. We worried constantly about them but God was good and they survived. Early in the war years I met a handsome, blond airman called Peter and fell in love. We married in 1940 and the following year we had a dear little baby girl with bright blue, searching eyes. She was a lively companion for me during the remainder of the war years as Peter had to go off to India and other battle areas.

The post war years were a time of difficulties and readjustments for the returned servicemen; they took time to settle down. Many of them had visited lands in Europe, the Middle East and the Far East. They were restless and unhappy about some of the conditions in England. Peter and I had two more baby girls over the next few years, but he never really settled or felt happy about his career. Then, suddenly he was offered a post in Kenya. He was very excited about the prospects and challenge that Kenya could offer. However, this was the time when Jomo Kenyatta, as leader of the Kenya African Union, was creating a political disturbance there and Mau Mau activities had already commenced.

It took courage to leave one's secure, native land to venture into an unknown colony, especially an unsettled one. Sensing his earnest desire to take up the post, I said we would go, provided he could convince me that the children would be safe. So it was decided he would go ahead for three months in order to assess the situation. The rest followed and became the history of our life in Kenya.

CHAPTER THREE

KENYA - HISTORY, LAND AND PEOPLE

There were pioneer souls that blazed their paths
where highways never ran. (S. W. Foss)

So many tales have been told, and so many books have been
written about East Africa, which is not surprising, as through the
centuries it has had a most turbulent history. Always, there were the
invaders such as Turks, Persians, Arabs and Portuguese. Bloodthirsty
battles were fought along its coastline, African tribes fought over land
and cattle, and the Arab traders terrorised the African inhabitants. Yet
this area is climatically favoured, has large areas of fertile land and
some of the most breathtakingly beautiful landscapes in the world.
Plus, of course, a unique wildlife. It seems impossible to believe that
a place so blessed could not have stilled the savage breasts of so many
invaders and inhabitants over such a long period of time. This sorry
state of affairs went on until the late 19th and early 20th centuries
when Germany took over what is now Tanzania (Tanganyika), and
Britain declared a Protectorate over Kenya. Britain also had interests
in Uganda as a neighbour of Egypt. Today, these countries are part of
the third world of independent nations.

From the 1500's the Portuguese, Turks and Arabs ruled the
coastline of Kenya. In the 1880's Seyid Said, the Sultan of Zanzibar
granted a concession to the British to administer justice, government
and collect taxes. Several times before this he had requested Britain to
take over, as from 1845 when he signed an anti-slavery treaty with the
British, he had begun to lose political influence. He also faced a
serious economic decline from the gradual decrease of the lucrative
return from the slave trade. Later, with the abolition of the legal status
of slavery, the social and economic life was badly affected. He was
also having difficulty in controlling the Mazrui Arabs along the
coastline. In 1840 he had captured Mombasa and this split the Mazrui
in two halves leaving one ruling in the north and the other to the
south. He established himself in Zanzibar with connections in
Mombasa. The Mazrui were long standing rivals of the Sultan's
family and both families had originated in Muscat.

Britain was not interested in this part of East Africa at that time and did not become involved. As early as 1826 the Foreign Office refused the request of the local Arabs to establish a Protectorate at Mombasa, but they did appoint a British Agent and Consul, John Kirk, at Zanzibar in 1841. This was to protect their interests in India as many British Indian traders had set themselves up in Zanzibar and along the East African coastline. They also wished to have good relations with the Sultan as he was the Sultan of Oman too and so held a strategic position on the overland route to India. The British Navy sailed in East African waters to suppress the slave trade and so did the German Navy.

John Kirk worked hard to secure close relations with the Sultan. Britain remained disinterested in East Africa and large areas were acquired by Germany. The Anglo German Agreement of 1886, however, divided areas into British and German spheres but Britain was still reluctant about any expansion. Two years later, in 1888, they did agree to the Sultan's concession and the British East Africa Company was given the task of administering the coastline and the interior of Kenya.

The British East Africa Company was grossly under-financed. With a skeletal staff they struggled to set up posts at Teita, Machakos and later at Kikuyu. They struggled constantly to get their caravans through but existed for only a few short years. Beyond Kikuyu they knew nothing of the country or its tribes. At least they had secured a route towards Uganda. In 1895 the British Government was forced to step in and declare a Protectorate over the territory. The Sultan of Zanzibar was recompensed for the surrender of a lease on a 10 mile wide strip of the coastline which the East Africa Company had held.

Very few explorers had ventured into the interior of Kenya. They had been put off by Arab tales of the ferocity of the Masai tribe who harried large areas taking cattle and women. They constantly attacked the Kikuyu and Kamba tribes driving them back from the plains into the hills; their people lived in great fear. The Kikuyu and Kamba retaliated but the Masai chiefly held the plains. After the declaration of the Protectorate the Foreign Office gave a directive to their Commissioner that as far as opportunities allowed they wanted to develop trade, to secure safer movement of traders and travellers, and without undue interference with tribal governments, native habits and customs to bring to the people the benefits of civilisation. With the slave trade now suppressed they expected prosperity.

The early days were not easy; the British Government had paid out huge amounts in grants. The Mazrui at the coast had rebelled and were suppressed by military action. Human porterage to up country areas had cost a fortune. However, by the end of the century a peaceful atmosphere prevailed.

The British built schools and hospitals for the Africans in order to educate them and take care of their health. They built dams and taught them soil conservation and how to cultivate the land. More missionaries arrived to teach them Christianity to help overcome their old fears of witchcraft and superstitions. They opened schools and artisan workshops and later brought out doctors and erected clinics and hospitals. A railroad was then built to open up the country. Britain brought in Asians to help in this gigantic task as there was no experienced labour. There were many tales of the endurance and terror experienced by these engineers and workmen. The book, "The Man-eaters of Tsavo", relates the terrifying experience of man-eating lions attacking and killing men at night-time. The building of the railroad was a tremendous achievement. When it was completed the Asians stayed on to trade. The first settlers also began to arrive.

Around the turn of the century there had been an outbreak of influenza in Kenya which was totally unknown there previously. Thousands of Africans had died, thus the land which had been claimed by the Kikuyu, Kamba, and Masai, depending on which tribe was temporarily dominant at the time, appeared deserted. In their search for a good place to live, the settlers found this quiet area very appealing. They hailed the countryside westward from Limuru as..."England with an eternal summer". They chose this land, bought their blocks and erected their first modest homes in these primitive surroundings. They cleared the bush and irrigated the soil. The Africans helped in the cultivating and were taught how to use a plough and sow seeds. When they saw the fruit of this labour they were very happy and there was good feeling between them and the settlers. Settlers' wives were very brave and worked hard to make a permanent home. In their lonely existence they hoped to rear a family who would carry on. The greater number of these people were easy going and kind and were fond of the Africans.

Two wars interrupted this happy state. In World War I the Kenyan men, black and white, fought together to combat the German forces of Tanganyika (now Tanzania) as Tanganyika was ruled by Germany at that time. After World War II, in which again the Africans fought along with the British, more settlers arrived in Kenya; farmers, engineers, architects and road builders. Large ranches, farms, coffee estates, tea estates, sugar and sisal estates, large tracts of wheat lands and some industry thrived and provided the country's economy. Kenya became self-supporting.

But now, into this stable state for all races, came the radical Mau Mau uprising, which covered the period from the late forties up to 1956. By the early sixties the winds of change were blowing in Africa and by 1963 Kenya was handed over by the British to the Africans. Colonial rule was short-lived - a mere sixty odd years.

The long-standing belief by the Kikuyus that Europeans had "stolen" their land had caused violence in 1922 when Harry Thuku led a riot in Nairobi. The, then, Government set up a Kenya Land Commission which eventually produced a report disallowing some Kikuyu claims, but suggesting additions to some of their holdings. They did not agree to this and later in 1934 they sent Jomo Kenyatta to London to put forward their case. As a child Jomo Kenyatta had been treated by doctors at a Presbyterian Mission in Kenya and was brought up and educated there. He married and had two children, Peter and Margaret. When he went to London he did not achieve any success but he attended the London School of Economics where he met many radical Africans. He married an English woman and had another son, also named Peter. He also paid visits to Russia. The outbreak of World War II trapped him in England. When he returned to Kenya in 1947 the Nationalist Movement in Africa was very strong. He became leader of the Kenya African Union. After this the Mau Mau was secretly formed and had been in existence for some time when suddenly these terrorists committed atrocious murders, chiefly of Kikuyus who were resisting the Mau Mau oaths, and some Europeans. Kenya was unprepared. In 1952 the government was forced to declare a state of emergency. After this declaration more Europeans on lonely farms and thousands of Africans were slain. When we heard of the way these people died we found it extremely upsetting. Jomo Kenyatta was arrested, tried and convicted as being leader of the Mau Mau. Later he was sent to detention in the Northern Frontier District along with five other Mau Mau supporters. After he was convicted, an avenge attack was made by the Mau Mau on the peaceful village of Lari and it was almost wiped out. They set fire to the houses one night and as the inhabitants ran out of their homes they were hacked to pieces with sharp bladed pangas, the Mau Mau's chief weapon. The bodies were unmercifully mutilated and unborn babies were cut from their mothers' wombs.

The Mau Mau leaders were educated men. The terrorists, in the main, were uneducated peasants who had succumbed to the instincts of their fore-fathers and their passion for witchcraft and secret societies. Oath taking had been a binding part of their lives and so they accepted that this was the way to recover the land where Europeans now lived, but their primitive lusts evolved into a blood bath.

The Mau Mau oaths were dreadful beyond belief. Records reveal that at the initiation ceremonies they chewed human remains and drank the blood of man and beast mixed with disgusting contents. They had intercourse with animals. The arch of entwined sugar cane or banana leaves through which the noviciates passed was adorned with the eyes of animals and sometimes the genitals of man and beast. Live cats and dogs were often nailed to the altar. They swore to bring the head of a European, to denounce Christianity, etc., etc. There were degrees of initiation, according to the rank they would carry in the society. The ones they had to perform at higher levels are too obscene to describe.

The land the Kikuyu claimed was the deserted land the early settlers had seen on their arrival; the land which had been fought over for so long by the Masai, Kikuyu and Kamba tribes. The Kikuyu were the only tribe to complain about stolen land despite the fact that they held the most beautiful, fertile land in Kenya. Offers of other land by the government were turned down as they said that the "spirits" would be against them there. The Masai and Kamba did not complain. However, only 20% of the land had been set aside for white settlement and farming.

Frustration and great financial losses were suffered by the settlers in the early years. Many of them were financially ruined. Their blood, sweat and tears through times of drought, locust plagues, the knowledge they had to learn the hard way of combating disease of land, animals and the human body, plus the depression years were a devotion to the country and its natives. They could not be termed exploiters for they gave a gigantic contribution of development. They brought the land to a state where it yielded rich crops and eventually reared grade cattle and sheep. The Kikuyu gained knowledge from this and were able to improve their own herds.

Prior to the last war Kenya received no aid from Britain - the policy was for the colony to be self-supporting. Men like Colonel Grogan and Lord Delamere injected fortunes into the land and suffered great losses. Other farmers, business men and entrepreneurs raised contributions. The first white hunters started the famous East African safaris and raised revenue for game licences from rich Americans and others. Settlers paid rates and taxes and the Africans paid a poll tax. There were never more than 30,000 whites in Kenya in our time. The Indians outnumbered them four to one and there were some 7,000,000 Africans. Today the Kenya population has risen to 28,000,000 approximately.

The Mau Mau was almost exclusively Kikuyu and the other tribes of Kenya were not affected. They were the people who worked and helped the country to survive during the dark years up to 1956. The coastal areas were considered safe and no atrocious acts were committed there.

With Jomo Kenyatta in jail the remaining Mau Mau leaders carried on. There was a lot of unrest and mopping up by the security forces. Troops were sent out from Suez and Britain to help. All Kikuyu males were rounded up and sent to jails and various camps which were being prepared to hold them so that screening tests of their loyalties could be carried out. Mau Mau members fled into the forests of the Aberdare Mountains and the slopes of Mount Kenya, but they still managed to communicate with others hiding in the city. They carried out attacks at night on lonely farms and killed and mutilated the stock of farmers. They stole food and other essentials for their existence in the wilds.

Eventually, in 1954, the security forces managed to break their lines of communication. Small groups of these security forces blackened their bodies, faces and hair with make up. They dressed and acted as Mau Mau and bravely entered the forests to set up ambushes.

They could speak Kikuyu as some of them had grown up on farms and had Kikuyu children as playmates. They were known as the "pseudo gangs". The forests with their thick almost impenetrable undergrowth, shrubs and trees, the wild animals and the freezing nights at high altitude were some of the hazards they staunchly faced plus the chance of being mistaken for real Mau Mau. It was a long and arduous task until 1956 before the uprising was finally defeated when the Englishman, Ian Henderson, captured Dedan Kimathi, the last Mau Mau leader at large.

As things settled down rehabilitation of the Kikuyus commenced. The great fear of the interned ones who had taken Mau Mau oaths resulted in many years of gradual release and de-oathing ceremonies were even held to try and help them overcome this fear.

PEOPLE

The indigenous people of Kenya are descended from Hamitic, Nilo Hamitic, and Bantu ancestors. The ones of Arabic and Egyptian origin include such tribes as the Masai, Somali, Nandi, Kipsigis, Suk, Luo, Karamajong and Turkana. With the exception of the Masai who wander over the south, south east and Rift Valley areas, and the Somali who are interspersed in Nairobi and the farming areas, the rest of these tribes are found in the areas around the western hills and the shores of Lake Victoria and in the north. The Bantu, who are a mixture of Negroid and Hamitic, include Kikuyu, Embu, Meru and Kamba who inhabit the central provinces of Kenya. There are many smaller tribes, off-shoots of these groups, and these intermarried with the Arabs along the coastline and include the Giriama, Swahili and Ndorobo. The Kikuyu is the largest tribe with Luo the second largest. These two tribes have a history of rivalry and today many of them hold important positions in government, professional and industrial fields.

When we arrived in Kenya the immigrants mainly consisted of British, Italian, Greek, Scandinavian, Pole, Jewish, Indian and Goan. They all took their part in the building up of the country. Some of the Indians owed allegiance to the Aga Khan who is a regular visitor to Kenya. He and his grandfather are responsible for the erection of many schools, hospitals and other buildings for their community.

THE LAND

We thought it was a miracle, after only 50 odd years of colonial rule, for the country to have reached the state it was in after so many dramatic struggles. We found it a land of contrasts, roughly the size of France, with varied climates, altitudes and scenery. It was to fascinate us all our days there. In the North it is bordered by Ethiopia and the Sudan, in the South by Tanzania, West by Uganda and Lake Victoria and in the East by Somalia and the glorious Indian Ocean.

The north is austerely lovely, though semi-desert and arid, with Beau Geste forts, wild animals, camels and donkeys. There too, is Lake Rudolph, famous for its big game fishing, where the diminishing tribe of El Molo live.

The south west is still untamed, a pastoral region for wild animals and wandering Masai with their herds of cattle. Mount Kilimanjaro, just over the border in the south east is the jewel which Kenya shares, for it can be seen from long distances north.

East lies the luscious tropical coast with white beaches unsurpassed in beauty, with their fringes of palm, mango, paw paw and banana trees, all sheltered by a friendly reef.

The west carries its atmosphere of days gone by when explorers and missionaries delved deeply into Africa and discovered the source of the Nile.

The land slowly rises from the coast through dry bush land, dotted with thorn and baobab trees, the home of elephants, rhinos, lions, leopards and many other animals and birds. Gradually, one hundred miles or so from present day Nairobi more fertile land appears which is suitable for farms and fruit growing.

Nairobi, which lies at approximately 5500 ft. altitude, was built on a swamp when a halt had been called to wait for more materials to arrive when the railroad was being built. It grew like 'Topsy' with Indian traders moving in to open a bazaar. Later, hotels sprung up such as the Norfolk, where settlers enjoyed their social visits to town, a break from their lonely existence in the bush. Nairobi was very small when we arrived but today it is a modern city with skyscrapers, wide, tree-lined streets, parks, a racecourse, a famous museum, a splendid university and large government buildings. On the outskirts of the city is the National Game Park where visitors can view, from close proximity in their vehicles, most of the indigenous wild animals in natural surroundings.

Travelling westward from Nairobi are the beautiful areas of Kabete, Kiambu and Limuru in the hills where coffee is grown. From Limuru it is a short drive to the great Rift Valley of Africa which splits Kenya, an awe inspiring sight. Along its floor are a string of lakes, home of flamingos and many other water birds, a fabulous carpet of pink as one approaches the shores. The volcanoes, Suswa and Longonot add to the scenic splendour, raising their heads above the smaller hills surrounding the lakes. Italian prisoners of war built a new escarpment road down the steep side of the Rift Valley during the last war and then at the foot they built a miniature church to commemorate their presence there.

Further west, on the far side of the Rift Valley is the farming centre of Nakuru, a neat market town with its lake of the same name. The town is backed by Meningai crater, and the lake by smaller hills. Lake Nakuru is world famous for its prolific bird life and wild life conservationists visit it regularly. In the Rift Valley itself are other famous lakes such as Naivasha and Elmenteita. Lord Delamere was the first man to settle near Lake Elmenteita. He set up large ranching areas and dairy farms. On the rim of the Rift at high altitude, other settlers cultivated land for wheat growing. These people struggled and prospered and their homes were in scenically splendid positions backed by the Aberdare range of mountains.

Beyond Nakuru, to the west, lie the impressive country areas of Njoro, Molo and Mau Summit at altitudes over 7000ft. In their rolling green hills were more dairy and sheep farms and forests. To the south west are Kericho, the large tea growing area and Kisii famous for its soapstone. From there the land slowly falls to the shores of Lake Victoria where one finds Kisumu, the chief port. There is a thriving fishing industry, the fish most prolific being tilapia which is very delicious fare. There is great activity in the harbour with the constant movement of fishing vessels, lake steamers carrying passengers and other smaller craft. The lake is an amazing spectacle, large as an inland sea. The area is malarial and the climate hot and very humid.

North-east of Kisumu are more tea estates at Nandi and Tinderet in the hills. Leaving Kisumu the lake veers into Ugandan territory and the road to the north connects with the main Kenya/Uganda highway. At this junction turning east, one arrives at the small towns of Kitale and Eldoret with the Northern Frontier District lying to the north. Here were more farms, ranches and wheat lands. South Africans trekked up to these parts early in the century. These small towns could tell many tales of former days and characterise the immigrant inhabitants who settled there. Many of them left in harder days. A road runs south from Eldoret to Timberoa, a forested area, and then on to the small hamlet of Equator where a notice-board informs one that you are now on the equator.

Leaving Nairobi to travel through the central provinces, Thika is the first small town where the Chania Waterfall and Fourteen Falls provide a spectacular show. Fort Hall follows, a stronghold in Mau Mau days held by a staunch and loyal supporter of the British, Chief Njiri. Then on to Nyeri which leads the way to Nanyuki and the perpetually snow-capped Mount Kenya (Kayeena and Kerinyagga are the Kamba and Kikuyu names for 'tail of the ostrich' used to describe Mount Kenya's peaks).The country was named after the mountain and Mount Kenya was thought to be the abode of 'God' in Kikuyu folklore. Many international mountain climbers attack its slopes and peaks. Facing Mount Kenya is the old Mawingo Hotel, later named the Mount Kenya Safari Club, a beautiful haven of peace associated with William Holden, the film star. Wild animals roam in the foothills of Mount Kenya, and there are many trout streams where fishermen can stay in attractive fishing lodges. The Nyeri and Nanyuki countryside is very beautiful as one can imagine. Large coffee estates, ranches and farms thrived there. Here too is the Lodge which the Government gave to Princess Elizabeth in which she was staying when her father died and she became Queen. Treetops Hotel, the famous tourist attraction, is close by.

All these areas of Kenya with their varying climates and altitudes provide fantastic vacation places and today tourists marvel at the choices offered. Through the years many Game Lodges have been erected where wild animals are prevalent. These are attractive in design and have top class accommodation.

Into this fascinating land, one June evening, the female members of the Ellis family stepped down from the aircraft which had flown them so many miles from England, and trod on the soil of Nairobi which was to be their new home.

CHAPTER FOUR

OUR NEW HOME

Our aircraft had landed at Eastleigh Airport, a small RAF station which was also used by commercial planes in those days. It was very spartan - just a few wooden huts being used for immigration facilities etc., with one acting as bar and restaurant, but it was cosily intimate and for several years we visited it when meeting or seeing off friends and have spent many happy moments there. Today, Nairobi has a much smarter international type airport which is used by almost every airline in the world.

As Peter, my husband, bundled us, plus luggage into the car he had waiting, we were all very curious as to what we would find in our new surroundings. Despite our fatigue, the children and I were very excited as we drove through the not very inspiring area of outer Eastleigh. I must confess as I viewed the drab housing and littered streets I felt a little apprehensive. The pungent odours of curry and refuse hung heavy in the air. I was to learn later that this road from the airport into town was a den of iniquity at night when beautiful Somali girls rushed out from their shacks to surround male motorists' cars, offering themselves for as little as twenty five cents. It was strange to see only African and Indian children playing and my eldest daughter's eyes grew large and thoughtful, as she said,

"Are there any English children here, Mummy?"

"Yes dear," I assured her, "there are many people and children living here and you will soon have lots of new friends."

Soon we turned into another road from which we branched off into the suburb of Muthaiga, very neat and smart in comparison. I didn't know it then, but this was a rather elite suburb, mostly populated by rich business people and consular officials. The houses were large and imposing. My husband had been allocated one of these by his company for six months until we had time to look round for a place of our own. We passed the British High Commissioner's home and turned in at the next driveway. My husband watched my reaction with an amused grin on his face. I am sure he was very proud to be showing us such a lovely first home in Kenya, for there as we pulled up was a very attractive double storey house with a large garden and a tennis court.

Standing outside the front pergola were three African servants lined up waiting to greet us. They looked very smart and clean, their skins shone and their smiles were wide and friendly as we stepped out of the car. We were introduced to John the house servant, Edward the cook and Opondo the garden boy.

"Jambo memsahib, jambo watoto" (Hello Madam, hello children), they all chorused as they grabbed our luggage and disappeared inside, laughing and excited at our arrival.

"Come along," said Peter, "I'll show you the garden a moment before it gets dark and then I have a surprise for you."

The garden was delightful - with large lawns, shrubs and colourful flower beds. Creepers adorned the walls of the house and a glorious pink rambler rose and a mauve petria blossomed round the pergola. The "surprise" bounded out of the kitchen door as we returned to the house - two surprises in fact, a large Alsatian and a little Dachshund who were introduced as Robby and Hobson. Peter explained that he had agreed to look after them as their owners had gone on six months long leave to England. The dogs were very friendly, being used to children. They scampered round the garden, and us, and in the process we received lots of slobbery lickings and lashes from Robbie's excited tail. On entering the house I caught sight of a large dining room and staircase before John ushered us into a huge English style lounge where we found a tray of refreshing tea and cakes waiting for us.

That was a lovely evening; the children went off to bed after deciding who would have which bed. Peter and I had a quiet dinner by candlelight superbly cooked by Edward. We found later that he was a natural cook, a rare find in Africa. As we started the meal, Peter placed a gun by the side of his plate on the table. At the sight of this I was shocked into the reality that we were in a place of danger. He reassured me that this was only a routine procedure, a safety precaution practised by most men at this hour as the Mau Mau's routine proved they made attacks on lonely farm houses when the servants were busy with the evening meal, forcing entry through the kitchens and so into the dining-rooms, catching the people unawares. He said there had been no such attacks in Nairobi and it was most unlikely there would be, but one should be alert and sensible about the situation. For years, when later we moved out to country areas, he always sat facing the kitchen door at dinner time with the gun at his side, as did so many of our friends and neighbours. I'm sure it was a deterrent against attack as one's own servants would pass on the word that their Bwana was armed and ready to fight any invaders.

Despite the gun episode, I was blissfully content as I drifted off to sleep that night in my new home with my husband, three children, three servants and two dogs. Our family has somewhat enlarged, I smilingly thought.

"How's your Swahili?" enquired Peter next morning. "Did you manage to learn any before you left England?"

Like most husbands, he was oblivious of how much time is needed to look after three children, sell up a home, pack everything, visit relatives, have inoculations, medical check-ups and the added anxiety of having one child rushed into hospital for an appendectomy, which is what happened to me during our three months alone. I confessed that I could only say 'hello', 'how are you', 'good-bye' and count to ten and that was it.

"Oh dear," he laughed, "You'd better get the book out because when I go to work in a couple of days time only the children will be speaking English!"

This was very true as very few servants in those days spoke English and we found it so at breakfast when Edward and John tried to hold long conversations with the children and myself, only to receive our blank embarrassed stares in return. They found this highly amusing and later we could hear them giggling in the kitchen at our inability to comprehend their language.

For two days, we spent a happy time exploring our home and

Nairobi. The city was not very large then but it had the attraction as you drove in of a dual highway bordered by palms, bougainvillaea, petria and other flowering shrubs and trees. At intervals were roundabouts where roads led into the city from the suburbs. These roundabouts were a splendid example of a City Council Parks Department really devoted to the task of making its city beautiful, for they were adorned with all kinds of shrubs and cacti, bordered by flower beds which were planted seasonally; gorgeous splashes of colour met our eyes. We found the Norfolk Hotel and the New Stanley Hotel which have been mentioned in so many books about East Africa. The New Stanley with its famous Grill Room and Long Bar where pictures of notable settlers adorned the walls. Both these hotels had large and interesting murals behind their bars of early settler scenes. The Old Torrs Hotel too we found attractive with its wooden staircase and panelled walls. One entered the old colonial atmosphere in all these places where the staff were alert, well trained and knew the whims and respected the wishes of all who entered. In their white kanzus, red sashes and fezes, they moved around quietly and cheerfully, taking great pride in their work.

We visited the Bazaar area, a mass of Indian dukas (stores), quite bewildering to a newcomer. One could spend hours browsing and never cease to be amazed at the variety of goods they stocked - from a safety pin to a new dress, from brass ware, ornaments, carvings to pots of paint and hardware, foodstuffs, jewellery, toys, shoes, floor coverings and, if one did not have what you needed, the owner would dash next door and procure it in a matter of minutes. Their service was overpowering and people could so easily be tempted to buy things they really had no intention of doing on entering. Bargaining, of course, came into this, something we had to get used to, and in the days to come we found very often, to our annoyance, that we could have bought some things much cheaper by more lengthy argument! A novel experience after shopping in England.

Then there was the Municipal Market with its stalls of flowers, fruit and vegetables, meat, fish and curios. It was a delight to carry home huge armfuls of flowers which were ridiculously cheap and irresistible; gladioli, asters, iris, marigolds, sweet peas, roses, carnations and many others to beautify one's home, which also saved robbing one's own flower beds. Nowhere else in the world have I seen such an abundance of flowers. Africans also sold them on the pavements in many areas bringing them into the city early in the morning from places like Limuru. Vegetables were cheap and plentiful. Fruits foreign to us such as paw paw, pineapple, mangoes, guavas were there for us to sample and avocado pears became a firm favourite once we acquired their taste. The meat was good as Kenya was a great agricultural country with plenty of beef, pork and delicious Molo lamb. Fish from the lakes and sea was there in great variety.

The central area had more conventional shops but most of these were also run by Indians, causing me to remark,

"Goodness, are there no European owned shops in Nairobi?"

In fact there were very few. The Indians did such a good job in this area, and would have been very stiff competition for their white cousins, so had been left with the monopoly on this kind of trade. The Europeans were usually employed by the various government departments or in the bigger manufacturing and engineering companies, or they were farming and growing tea and coffee, Peter explained.

We toured the government buildings such as the Law Courts and City Hall, saw Government House, another replica of Empire, equally as gracious as any in the world, visited the Museum (very small then) but no less interesting to us. It was to become very famous owing to the efforts of Dr. Louis Leakey and his family. We discovered three cinemas and two small theatres. Later we found these theatres provided very good entertainment, one of them importing professional actors and actresses from London who produced a new play every six weeks or so. The other one was used by one professional producer and other local amateur groups who did a splendid job putting on terrific shows over the years, such as "The Boyfriend", "Salad Days", "Mame", "South Pacific", Oklahoma", "Fiddler on the Roof" and many others, providing a very pleasant social evening as one usually preceded a visit to these by dinner in the company of friends.

There were no high rise buildings at that time and some areas could hardly be called smart. Wooden huts were used as government offices in some cases, and many buildings had corrugated iron roofs, but this was offset by tree-lined streets of palms, jacarandas, oleanders and more bougainvillaea, with picturesque mosques rising majestically here and there to dispel any drabness. A charming old church with a steeple decorated the highway on the way into town which was the Catholic Cathedral. In this area there were two other quaint churches, plus the ordinary towered Anglican Cathedral.

The suburbs consisted of European areas where one caught glimpses through the trees of Tudor style homes, modern houses, touches of Italian, Swedish or Greek architecture and even a modest version of Versailles. The buildings were mostly of stone and looked solid, sound and secure. The Sikhs were the fundis or craftsmen of Kenya and a very good job they made of erecting houses or making furniture. The Indian areas alternated from poorer class houses and blocks of flats, also of stone, to the colourful villas of the more prosperous. African housing consisted of small houses and large blocks of flats. These were allocated in locations to those working for various companies or for the government.

Unfortunately, there were many unsightly slum areas on the outskirts of town where Africans had erected makeshift homes from any materials they could lay their hands on, such as flattened petrol cans, old pieces of timber and corrugated sheeting, hessian and even cardboard. This was chiefly due to young men coming in from country areas to the big city to try to find employment and to satisfy their curiosity as to a so called more modern way of life. It was impossible, of course, but despite their disillusionment they stayed and grew in numbers taking jobs when available or seeking help from their relatives already employed. These areas were a potent health hazard. The Government was forced to bulldoze them regularly after warning the inhabitants, but they continued to reappear.

Good hospitals and schools were also there to complete all the needs of a new family, so I felt reasonably content with our surroundings as we returned home at the end of the second day.

Of course, many things were strange to both myself and the children. Because of security, children were not allowed to roam away from their own gardens. This was really no hardship as gardens varied in size from one to five acres so that exercise was not restricted. Adults travelled everywhere in cars as again it was not considered safe to walk on lonely roads. Tastes and smells were different; the air was full of dust, pollen and the aroma from tropical shrubs and flowers. Houses smelt cleanly of furniture polish as the African servants used this to excess on furniture and wooden parquet floors, a chore which they seemed to really enjoy as they polished the floors by means of sheepskin pads attached to their feet. They whizzed around singing and laughing like professional ice skaters. The result was worth the effort as most floors shone like glass. These lovely parquet floors were usually adorned with colourful Persian rugs.

The sight seeing days were a lovely holiday interlude, far too short, but now we had to get down to every day life and settling in.

CHAPTER FIVE

SETTLING IN

Peter was loath to leave us next day as he had really enjoyed showing us around. As he drove away, I knew that I must really get down to learning Swahili as he had been giving all the orders for meals and duties in the house and garden. That first day was quite an experience as my powers of miming failed to impress John, Edward or Opondo. I carried my "Teach Yourself Swahili" book around and struggled valiantly to learn a word or a phrase at a time.

I was grateful to receive my first visitor mid-morning, our neighbour, Marie, who called to say hello and to ask if she could help in any way. Marie was a nursing sister who had come out from Scotland to work at Nairobi Hospital. She had met Gavin, an engineer, and now they were married with two small children. She was to prove a great friend and it was not long before we had an opening made in the garden hedge so that we could step through quickly to each other's houses. She was sensible, practical, yet had an impish, dry humour which appealed to me greatly.

Understanding my problem of communication with the staff, she immediately volunteered to be my interpreter for a few weeks, otherwise she said I would really be led a dance! As we sat at coffee, she told me funny tales of misunderstood Swahili, such as when the lady of the house thought she had ordered potato soup for dinner, only to find her husband's boots bubbling away in the pan. The Swahili word for potatoes is "viazi" and for boots "viatu". She had obviously used the wrong one and the cook was left wondering why this crazy lady wanted the bwana's boots boiled! Another was where a party was being held up country, the main dish being sucking pig. The lady of the house said to the servant,

"Now when I call for you to bring it through, I want you to quickly decorate it and put this apple in its mouth."

When the moment came, the African appeared with the delicious steaming hot fare on a tray, but the apple was in his mouth instead of the pig's! Of course, we were to learn that the African, on the whole, is a great comedian.

Maureen, Valerie and Elaine, our three girls, were delighted to have a holiday at home until we could arrange for their schooling and spent their time playing games and chasing round the garden with the dogs. They had found a tree house in a large tree behind the tennis court, plus some ready made swings, so they were fully occupied.

One morning John came to me, looking very strained and very serious. He reeled off a whole spate of Swahili which contained the word 'choka' several times. Still not understanding much of the language, I sent for Marie who informed me that he was saying he was tired and was asking for the help of an ayah to do the childrens' rooms and their washing and ironing.

"Goodness," I said, "surely we don't need four servants. Surely it can't be necessary."

Marie then told me that most people with children had an ayah and I knew she had one. She said that it was expected and that if I did not employ one life would probably become very difficult and that it was best to agree. There was a way of life to adhere to both from the European and African views. Later I was to look on it all as a mutual aid society, but one where we appeared to be the parents of a very large family, whether we liked it or not, or whether or not we could afford this number of servants.

And so Aminah arrived on the scene. She was a Kisii, rather serious, very clean and certainly efficient at her job. In the afternoons when she had three hours off duty, one could see her peddling away madly on her brand new, shiny bicycle down the driveway. I never knew where she went, also I never really saw her smile, yet she seemed fond of the girls and really kept them and their clothes spotless. I wondered if she had any personal problems, but if she did, she never spoke of them. And so the servant problem was solved and things went very happily and smoothly.

In the suburbs every house had its servants' quarters where the staff lived. They were erected in a corner of the garden, usually walled or hedged off from the main area and were good houses of stone, with tiled roofs and cement floors. Water and light were laid on, plus WC and shower. There would be a kitchen and then a room for each servant or sometimes two of them would have to share. Also there would be a small garden which they could cultivate, but not many did. The employer provided a bed, blanket, mattress and pillow, sometimes a table, chair and curtains. The rest the servants had to find themselves. We had to provide aprons and hats for them to work in during the day, and uniforms for evening and serving at table. These were the long white kanzus with which they wore a sash, embroidered waist-coat and a fez. Ayahs wore blue dresses, white aprons and hats, which were also provided. Rations were supplied to them weekly of maize flour, tea, sugar and meat and wages were paid monthly. These wages may have seemed small, but with most things provided for them, they were as much or more than most Europeans could afford. Some servants took food from the house too, but did not really look on it as stealing when taken to task. When remonstrating with them about theft being wrong, they would say,

"But memsahib, my relatives called to see me", or "But bwana, memsahib, you are my father and my mother!"

I remember one in particular who would take all the bread and sugar and leave me without any at crucial moments. One Sunday afternoon when I got unexpected visitors and found no sugar, I said to him,

"Now here is my sugar bowl. Would you please take it to your house and fill it with my sugar so that I can give my visitors tea."

"Oh yes, memsahib, of course I will," he beamed, and came dashing back with it, so happy to oblige!

Of course there were good and bad servants. We had one or two bad ones but others stayed with us for years at a time and shared our family life as we shared theirs. Usually the men came to town on their own leaving their wives and families at home in the country areas where their particular tribe lived.

Sometimes the family would come to town for a week or so to be with their husbands and fathers, but then they would return to look after the family stock and shamba (land). I thought it a lonely sort of life for them but they didn't seem to mind too much. Usually when the rains were due, (twice yearly in March and November), one's servants would all start asking for leave at the same time so that they could go home to help till the land and repair their huts. This could leave one in a predicament but we always coped one way or another.

We were now meeting more people and being invited to various homes, mostly through my husband's work. Some of the friendships formed in those days are still as strong as ever. There was a warmth and a caring for each other because we were few in an alien land, and the element of danger was ever present. Stories reached us of many atrocities. Early one evening we went to visit a family we knew at Dandora, planning to be home before darkness fell at 7pm. They lived in one of the Mowlem Construction Company's houses which were placed in a boma for safety reasons with guards at the gate. Outside was a swamp where it was known that Mau Mau members hid out during the daytime. As we arrived at the boma, we found that the police had decided to do a swoop on the area. They had surrounded the swamp and captured several Mau Mau, including one famous leader. When all was quiet we peeped over the fence to see the horrific sight of a dead English Police Inspector being carried to an ambulance. Also askaris were hustling Mau Mau prisoners into lorries. At the least sign of protest they were bashed indiscriminately with the butt of the African askaris' rifles. We felt shocked, upset and nauseated being so close to this affray.

Despite this event, our lives went on as usual. The girls were accepted at a school. All schools charged quite high fees to help with their upkeep. When the morning came for them to start I expected a few protests and perhaps even tears from the youngest, but the excitement of getting ready and Aminah's fussy attention of brushing their hair and even their clothes with a brush as they went out of the door, took their minds off what lay ahead. They were lucky to have each other's company. They looked very smart as they trotted off to the car. I have a photo of them somewhere which I took one day so I could send copies to the grandparents and which I captioned 'Three Little Maids from school are we!' Each morning from then on, Aminah would line them up after breakfast to inspect hair, clothes, shoes, etc. and always the clothes brush came into use. I confess that on return at lunch-time they did not look so smart or clean! They settled in very well for some time at their first school and quickly made friends who visited and stayed with us from time to time.

Social life for wives consisted of morning coffee parties, visits to sports clubs with friends, shopping trips in town and then there were dinner parties in each others' homes in the evenings, plus the theatre shows. So even though at first I expected to be bored with no household chores, I found this not to be the case. I soon had a circle of very good friends and the days flew by. The climate in Nairobi was almost perfect with daylight at 7am and darkness at 7pm. There were no seasons as such - just the rains and a colder spell in July/August, but we never had to wear an overcoat all our days there. Except for the colder months, we enjoyed an average daytime temperature of 78 - 80°F all year round.

Peter had to fly to Zanzibar for a few days. Cautioning me to really lock up well at night, he also said he had asked friends to call in or ring us now and again to check that all was well. The first night he was away I received a terrible fright. The children had gone to bed and the staff had left. Suddenly there was a loud banging on the French doors of the dining room. The dogs, Robbie and Hobson, were asleep on the floor of this room and never roused. I was petrified; I pulled myself together at the second loud banging and timidly pulled aside the curtain at one of the windows. I saw a very large Sikh gentleman in the khaki uniform of the East African Power and Lighting Company whom I knew. He said he was very sorry to disturb me but could he please use our phone to call his company regarding a power failure in the area. I could have sobbed with relief but managed to laugh instead. He was a very nice Sikh and after he had got the information he needed he profusely apologised for worrying me. I think he knew how badly he had scared me. After he left, I had to admit to myself that an underlying stress as to personal safety was definitely going to be part of our lifestyle especially after darkness fell. Reproachfully I told Robbie and Hobson what a wash out they were as guard dogs, for all they had done on waking was to wag their tails!

However, overall, we felt safe in Nairobi and did not envy our brothers in the country on their lonely farms and estates. They had powerful sirens installed in case of attack so that neighbours and police could hear them over long distances. They had a locked room for iron rations, ammunition and fire extinguishers, etc. The security forces were well trained; the army, police and an African homeguard worked together and did a tremendous job. We never doubted their ability to eventually control the situation.

I spent a great deal of time in the garden as I had always loved pottering around with flowers, plants and vegetables. The climate resulted in a continual supply of all these things. Necessity being a hard task master resulted in my quickly learning sufficient Swahili to cope with most eventualities. John, Edward, Opondo and Aminah became more impressed with my ability each day.

"You know Swahili very well Madam," was praise indeed. The children too picked up the language even quicker and we soon began to feel like old settlers.

CHAPTER SIX

OUR FIRST SAFARI

Soon the childrens' first holiday from school came round and as Peter was due to make a visit to Moshi in Tanzania, (then Tanganyika), we coaxed him into letting us accompany him.

This was to prove a real safari, travelling on dirt roads for part of the way. We left early one morning just after sunrise. The first twenty miles or so were on a tar sealed road to Athi River. Here, we branched off to the south on a dusty and stony track, which would take us to the little town of Namanga on the Tanganyika border, a further eighty miles away. What excitement it caused for us to see giraffe near Athi River, tall and stately, nibbling at the top branches of thorn trees, looking down at us disdainfully as if to say

"How dare you intrude on our morning meal."

A little later came hundreds of zebra, wildebeest, warthogs, all kinds of buck and ostriches, some just standing and staring at us curiously, others shooting off in all directions, tails in the air, causing a minor dust storm. It was a thrill hard to describe, a scene one felt imprinted on the mind rather than seen with the eyes. This was African magic; the blue sky, rolling plains, red earth, thorn trees, purple hills in the hazy distance, the sun glinting on the leaves of the trees and morning dewdrops on the grass, and these magnificent creatures feeding and leaping around in the land which was their birthright. We could have been a million miles from Nairobi and civilisation already, not a human in sight - just us and Africa.

It certainly took our minds off the bumpy road and the dust which came pouring into the car. It was useless to try and escape from this red dust of Kenya and we soon came to accept the fact that one always ended up looking an unbecoming shade of reddish-brown at the end of any such journey in the bush. Perhaps this was why the first Europeans who arrived in East Africa were known as the "Red Strangers".

As we travelled along across the open plain and through small dents in the hills where various rock formations fascinated us, we saw our first Masai. Some were young children tending cattle, others young males in their typical stance of standing on one leg, leaning on their long spears, heads erect and proud, a reminder of their ancestry; their hair dressed with red ochre and cow urine and wearing only a blanket which was draped across one shoulder. We drove into Kajiado, just a cluster of huts and a trading post where crowds of them surrounded our car, gazing in at the children, chattering unintelligibly. Wonderingly, they touched Elaine's hair which was bright gold. Luckily she was not scared and smiled back at them. They begged for cigarettes. We drank a Coca-Cola to quench our thirst, then escaped down the road.

Progress was slow for there was danger of damaging the car on the rough surface of the road so it was almost lunch time when we reached Namanga which was a green oasis backed by hills. As we entered the town over a bridge, we found on our right a small hotel which was surrounded by trees and shrubs. It had a thatched roof and a pleasant cool interior. The children discovered a large aviary in the garden full of brightly coloured birds, a joyous sight for them. We stayed for lunch which was most appetising, all the fruit and vegetables being fresh from the garden. The landlord was very friendly and hospitable. We were to find later many of these small hotels scattered throughout East Africa where the owners never forgot you once you had paid a visit. On future calls, you were welcomed as a good friend or relative.

More Masai appeared on the scene as we left. We tried to photograph them, but they became very agitated on sighting the camera so obviously were not in favour of this action and we left it. In years to come, they lost this fear and begged to have pictures taken, but they had learned to ask for payment in return!

We had now crossed the border into Tanganyika. The Customs barrier was just beyond the hotel and there ahead was a lovely tar sealed road stretching into the distance. The countryside here was very green, but of all shades of green, like a patchwork quilt. On our left were the foothills of Meru, an impressive mountain which stands sentinel over the town of Arusha which would be our next stop. It was a pleasure to whizz along after the previous rough passage. We were descending in altitude to about 4,000 feet so it became warmer and humid. As we approached Arusha, the scenery became more tropical, everything appearing so lush and green with palm, banana, and mango trees and brilliant shrubs in the suburban gardens.

Arusha is the small town where preparation for safaris to Ngorongoro Crater and Serengeti then took place. We stopped at the Arusha Hotel for a drink and met up with several of the old characters who provided the atmosphere for such films as "Hatari", "King Solomon's Mines" and "Mogambo". Hunters and guides were caught up in a whirl of activity, for such a safari was about to get on the road. This was very enthralling for us and we would have loved to participate, but instead we had to wave good-bye and take the road to Moshi.

This road runs parallel with the great Mount Kilimanjaro. Unfortunately, the two peaks were shrouded in cloud as we drove along through the shrub, and later sugar cane plantations and we could only see the foothills. Native huts were dotted amongst the shrubbery, where we caught glimpses of family life - the wives leaning over their cooking pots, children playing, goats and chickens wandering around the open spaces. They were happy; laughing, shouting, singing and waved at us as we went past.

Soon we came to Moshi, a small town of wide tree-lined streets, Indian dukas, hotels and a small industrial area. It was even warmer here, as we had again descended in altitude. There was a haze of dust in the air as some streets were not tar sealed. The local African women in their colourful cotton dresses and head scarves were preparing to pack up their wares as there had been a market in an open area. Now they would trek back to their homes in the country before the evening shadows fell.

We had to search in the suburbs for the home of the engineer who worked for my husband's company where we were to stay. We were so looking forward to a refreshing shower, some clean clothes and a rest from the journey, as the heat was foreign to us after the clear fresh air of Nairobi. However, this was not to be. When we found our friend, Dennis, he was a very worried man. His young wife had joined him from England only a few short weeks ago. Not realising she would be living in a malarial area, she had not taken any pills until too late and had gone down with cerebral malaria. Released from hospital, she was now back home, but was still a very sick and weak girl.

We insisted on finding accommodation at an hotel and I am sure he was relieved as three children would hardly have created a peaceful atmosphere. So back to town we went, only to find the rooms all taken, but we were directed to an old hotel out of town called "The Lion Cub" where blessedly they said we could camp out in two outside rooms which were pretty rough but at least had army beds in them. Darkness was now falling so any accommodation was most welcome. Mosquitoes turned out in full force and having just left poor Pamela I felt a little apprehensive about my childrens' welfare when I saw the mosquito nets for the beds had enormous holes in them. Looking back, I remember sewing away madly trying to join up these large holes by the light of a Tilley lamp in the dusty little room. What a chore! I missed dinner and crept into bed, unfed, unwashed and thoroughly exhausted, thinking so much for my first African safari!

At 6am, Peter roused us all shouting in through the open door,

"Wake up! Wake up! Come and see the mountain. It might not be out later."

We dashed out and looked up over the trees but saw nothing.

"Where? Where?", we all chorused.

"Not there," he said, "Higher. Look up higher, look up to the sky."

And there was Kilimanjaro, in all its glory, immensely startling, breathtakingly beautiful with the rising sun turning the snow on its summit into icing sugar pink. What a sight. I never forgot this first view of Kilimanjaro at close quarters, the wonder of beholding one of God's great scenic gifts to man.

We stayed in Moshi for a week and whilst Peter carried out his many duties during the day, I took the children for rides round the country roads exploring the lower slopes of the mountain. We found delightful waterfalls and stony brooks, where we paddled in the clear water, crossed picture book bridges and picnicked under shady trees. We visited sugar plantations and coffee estates and in the evenings visited homes where the local people entertained us royally. We also explored the dukas in town and bought souvenirs to take back home. The Indian owners also invited us to curry lunches. This friendly hospitality was all part of the comforting comradeship of those early days in East Africa. One felt part of a great family for, as I wrote earlier, these people never forgot you, even if they did not see you again for years.

All too soon it was time to retread the road to Nairobi. This first trip really made us aware of the great beauty and fascination of Africa and whetted our appetites for more journeys of exploration as soon as we could possibly make them.

CHAPTER SEVEN

"MITINI"

It was good to be back at home, but now we had to search for a place to live for our six months at Muthaiga was almost over. We were sad at the thought of leaving John, Edward and Opondo as they were the servants of the people coming back. Also, we would be saying good-bye to Robbie and Hobson, and I would miss my friendly neighbour, Marie, although we could still visit.

Not many houses were vacant in the city and we dreaded the idea of a flat. Just when we thought we would never find a suitable place, an advert appeared in the local newspaper offering a two year lease on a house at Lower Kabete; Kabete we knew was 5 or 6 miles out of town. We discussed the danger angle, but then decided to ride out one evening just for a look.

We found the journey from the city very beautiful, out through the suburbs, passing Spring Valley Police Station, and then across a wooded valley, where coffee estates appeared on the hillsides. There were some houses along the roadside so it was not really isolated. We soon turned right down a narrow lane called Taylor's Road where we had been told to look for the name board "Mitini". "Mitini" means "in the trees" in Swahili. I am not sure what we expected to find at this stage, but certainly not what we did. As we turned in at the gate there appeared 2 acres or so of parkland, - a carpet of vivid green lawn dotted with large shady trees of many varieties and along both sides of the driveway the widest herbaceous borders imaginable, which had obviously been created by a great and gifted gardener.

As we approached the house, we saw on the right a gigantic clump of bamboo, the largest I had ever seen, encircling which was a lawn and flower beds edged with bricks which formed a round-about for cars to drive in and out with ease. The drive itself carried on across the front of the long verandahed homestead and disappeared round the far end. It looked a very large house, which indeed it was, with white walls and red roof. There were gables at each end with large windows and opening on to the verandah, which connected the gables, were numerous windows and doors. Definitely a gentleman's residence.

"My goodness!" I said to Peter, "this is really a lovely place but I'm sure it will be very expensive."

An elderly gentleman appeared who came down the verandah steps to greet us. We were feeling hesitant as to whether we should even bother to look around, but he was so charming as he greeted us, asking us into his home, that we followed without a murmur.

"I'm so glad you have come," he said, "and I do hope you will like the place and be happy here, as happy and content as I have been."

Whereupon, he sat down and began to weep. We were so distressed to see him in this state and waited quietly for him to recover.

"I have made a few enquiries about you after you replied to my advert," he finally said, "and you have been highly recommended. You see I need someone rather special to leave here, as I am going away to England. My dear wife passed away recently and I cannot bear to go on living in a place with so many memories. I don't know how you will feel when I tell you this is not just a house but a 50 acre estate with the large house, a two bedroomed cottage which is let, two blocks of servants quarters, orchards, greenhouses, workshops, stables, and a pump house as the water is pumped from the river in the valley at the rear. There is also a large, lucrative vegetable area with overhead irrigation, a market garden in fact, and two rose gardens which provide roses for two shops and one hotel in town. There is a tennis court overgrown, I'm afraid, but it could easily be restored."

He paused a while, then carried on:

"The main house is quite large and also has a 2 bedroomed guest wing. Security is very good with Spring Valley Police Station so near and you have neighbours all round. There is a tenant in the guest house."

We kept very quiet.

"Now please don't let this frighten you off." he continued, "I would leave you the head gardener, Omalanya, and the twelve garden staff who would carry on as usual producing the flowers and vegetables for sale. The income from these makes a modest profit and also pays their salaries. Are either of you interested in gardening?"

I confessed that I loved gardens and that I had been brought up on a farm in the north of England where my grandfather had kept the most beautiful gardens, but that I had not anticipated living in anything other than an ordinary dwelling house in Kenya. Peter also emphasised that we had not expected to find such a large establishment. However Mr. Mitchell carried on to say that a Miss Carberry rented the cottage and that she was a very good tenant who would pay rent and water bills.

"Let me show you round anyway before it gets dark," he insisted.

Peter looked at me questioningly, but there seemed no way to escape as he eagerly led the way. What a show place it proved to be; orchards full of oranges, mandarins, grapefruit, avocado pears, bananas, and guavas; vegetables of all varieties, and the most magnificent roses and ferns; potting sheds with hundreds of potted plants all for sale; workshops where Omalanya made all the seed boxes and containers for hanging baskets etc. There was also all the machinery which would be left for use.

The interior of the house, though spacious and grand, was enticingly comfortable. At the end of the tour, however, we could only hesitate and say we would like a day or two to think it over. As we drove away, waving at his sad and lonely figure, we felt a pang of remorse that we could not say yes immediately to his offer. But there were so many aspects to consider and we were rather overawed by the responsibilities such a place would bestow upon us.

"It's no good", said Peter, " it will be far too much to cope with. You know how busy I am and I would never have enough time to devote to the place. It's very secluded too with all the surrounding gardens and forest. Would it be safe for the children? Also all the garden produce would need delivering. Who would do that? You can't drive and that would need time. We have no second vehicle yet. No, it's mad, I think we had better forget it."

I was inclined to agree with him. After all we only needed a house and it all seemed beyond our capabilities. The house too would need more servants and these we had yet to find.

"Still, it's a wonderful place," I said, "and it seems so sad that he must leave it. What a lot of pleasure he must have got from those fantastic gardens."

Peter glanced sideways at me for he knew how fond I was of gardening, but he didn't pursue the matter and so for a few more days we hunted for another house without luck. One morning Mr. Mitchell from "Mitini" rang us up to say would we please go out to see him again. He was leaving for England in a week's time. Had we made a decision yet?

"Well no we haven't Mr. Mitchell," I replied and went on to tell him our fears of taking the property.

"Please come out and discuss it further with me. You know it's not as awesome or difficult to handle as you believe. Please come."

This time we took the children. As we drove through the gates some strange power made us feel at home and we felt everything would be alright. We talked freely with Mr. Mitchell. He was kind and understanding, insisting that we should take the place as he felt we would care for everything. He wanted to just walk out saying he could not bear to touch anything.

"There are several items belonging to my wife. Can I ask you to handle that for me?"

Tears were very close and although I was appalled at the thought of everything being left I tried to be comforting.

"Of course I will do all I can for you Mr. Mitchell, but I cannot be responsible for all your lovely things. I will pack them all away for you in one of the stores until such time as you need them and I will use my own."

"I don't really care what happens you know," he answered, "nothing seems to matter."

"Oh, but it will, it will, in time, believe me," I consoled him, "you must go on remembering the happy times and soon you will rearrange your life. You may even want to return here some day."

"Do you think so?" he asked wonderingly.

"I'm sure of it. This lovely place will bring you back, you mark my words," I firmly replied.

I think I knew that life at "Mitini" would be a great experience and it certainly was. Looking back now on all our time in Africa, "Mitini" provided us with a style of life that was really "Kenya". It was far enough from the city to feel "country" and although it could not have been called a farm, it was near enough to pass for one, especially when later on we added dogs, horses, rabbits and poultry to our collection.

The children were very excited for they had loved Mitini immediately and we set to packing all our belongings for the big move. We interviewed prospective servants and chose a boy named Johan, who would be cook, another one, Andrea, who would clean and at the last minute when Aminah decided she did not want to live out of the city, we took a large, jolly girl called Teresina to take her place as ayah.

About this time, a young engineer called Johnnie Murphy and his wife, Doreen, had arrived in Kenya to work for my husband's company. They had not been able to find a house, so we offered to let them stay with us at Mitini in the guest wing for a while until they could get settled. They volunteered to help us with the move and so it was decided we would all move in on the same day.

The great moving day soon came along; we all exhausted ourselves fetching, carrying, placing furniture where it fitted in with the existing decor, making up beds, snatching a hurried meal or drink and introducing ourselves to all the garden staff and to Miss Carberry in the cottage. Finally, at 9pm, with the girls in bed and the servants gone to their quarters, we locked the many doors and windows carefully with a mind to security. Bed beckoned weary bodies when just on the point of saying good night to Johnnie and Doreen there came a loud banging on the dining room window. A voice we recognised as Johan's shouted,

"Bwana, Bwana, kuja, kuja pezi, iko shauri kubwa!"

We all froze as we felt an ominous, eerie silence about Mitini and its grounds now that it was dark. Peter went to the window and opened the latch to say,

"What is it Johan?"

"Kuja Bwana, kuja," followed by something that sounded to us like, "Bibi angu nakufwa shauri Mau Mau, shauri Mau Mau," as he went dashing off into the darkness. This translated meant 'come, come quickly bwana, here is a bad thing, my wife is dead. An affair of the Mau Mau.'

Peter looked at Johnnie saying, "Shall we see what is going on?"

"Oh, no," I stopped him, "please don't go outside. You know it may be a trick. Sometimes the Mau Mau get your servants to say something is wrong outside so that they can gain entry. It's really not safe and why has he gone dashing off like that. Why didn't he wait for you?"

"Yes," said Johnnie thoughtfully, "perhaps we should ring the police post before we venture out."

"Alright," said Peter, "you ring them girls. We'll just shine a torch out here and I will take my gun. We won't go beyond the back verandah until the police come."

They didn't do this as once outside they could hear all our servants chattering, shouting and even laughing. Peter shouted,

"Lock the door behind us. I think it's alright. We are just going to the quarters to see what's happening."

By this time Doreen had rung the police who were already on their way. When they arrived, we followed them through the shrubbery to the quarters where Johan's wife, stark naked, and it was a cold night, was being held by Johan on the ground under a garden tap with cold water pouring over her at full bore.

"Whatever in the world are you doing?" I remember shouting.

I saw Peter walking out of one of the rooms. He hurried over saying,

"Has she come round? Good Lord what a business. We had to break into her room where we found her unconscious on the floor. She had been cooking supper on a charcoal stove with all the windows and doors locked and no ventilation. The fumes knocked her out and she was almost dead. Johan was not shouting 'shauri Mau Mau', he was saying 'shauri moshi' (smoke)!"

At this stage, Mary, Johan's wife, started to moan and struggle away from the cruel lashing of water. Johan managed to get her onto her feet. I shouted for blankets and wrapped her up warmly. Johan and I then walked her up and down the path a little and gradually back to the house. We sat her on the laundry table and I asked Doreen to make lots of black coffee. Why is it that one's mind always goes blank in an emergency? I couldn't remember the right thing to do but hoped for the best when I kept lacing the coffee with brandy. I alternately walked her up and down and as she liked perching on the laundry table that was where she rested in between. As the stimulating drinks took effect, she started to chatter in a dialect we could not understand for she was from Kakamega.

"Thank God," I thought, "she's going to make it. What a terrible thing a death would be on our first night here."

Meanwhile Peter was apologising to the European Police Inspector, who was accompanied by two African Askaris, for bringing them out on a false Mau Mau alarm.

"Don't apologise," said Paddy Murphy, the Inspector, "it could have been a hoax and it's always best to be safe than sorry. I wanted to meet you anyway to tell you never to hesitate to call me if you have any suspicions of trouble. We patrol this area regularly because of the forest on your boundary. We also worry about Miss Carberry. I advised her to move into a flat in Nairobi but she won't hear of it; she has a loyal Kikuyu working for her and one of these days I'm sure the Mau Mau are going to have a go at him and she could quite easily become involved. Have a chat to her sometime."

As he started to leave, Mary burst into uncontrollable chatter interspersed with giggles, which we found infectious, as we all joined in laughing with relief.

"Don't overdo the brandy," said Paddy with a wry grin." I'd join her if I wasn't on duty. Don't let her go to sleep for a few hours though and keep her moving."

Now that his wife was safe Johan mysteriously disappeared, no doubt to creep into his bed. We tossed up as to who should stay with Mary first and it fell to my lot.

"Wake me up in an hour or two," Peter said anxiously "don't stay by yourself too long."

Mary undoubtedly grew more addicted to her "cure" as the night wore on and demanded further helpings at regular intervals; these I watered well down as her recovery became certain. Eventually she objected to walking around, preferring to squat on the table clasping her knees, gabbling incoherently - probably the story of her life or many other experiences.

As it became colder I too wrapped a blanket round my shoulders and partook of the "cure". The hours rolled by and I forgot or decided not to wake my relief, for by this time we were both engaged in animated conversation in our respective tongues. Mary leaned over and put her arm around me, gazed intently into my eyes, telling me, I'm sure, that I was her buddy for life.

This is how Peter found us at 5am, furious with me for not waking him. He marched Mary off to her husband's bed and then led me to mine where I passed out in a matter of seconds.

The children who had never heard a thing all night wondered why Mummy was not very agile and seemingly uninterested in exploring the estate next morning!

CHAPTER EIGHT

COUNTRY LIFE

What a hectic time those first days at Mitini were, but I stole a quiet moment to pack away the personal belongings of Mrs. Mitchell. A very sad task was the removal of personal cosmetics, spectacles, even passport from the dressing table. I paused to look out of the window at the beautiful garden and thought how she must have loved living here and how we should all enjoy each day for how quickly we can be taken away. I made a silent vow to her that I would cherish and care for her home; it almost seemed as if she could hear me and that I knew her, and I felt calm and peaceful.

My first duty, of course, was to the running of the gardens for how Peter chafed each morning at having to take large baskets of roses and ferns and deliver them to florists and hotels; poor chap, he had so many other things on his mind. So we bought a Ford van and I took driving lessons, but chiefly taught myself by driving it round and round our grounds. I also backed it through a garage door but that was my only casualty!

Omalanyo, the head gardener, was a god send. He was so organised at producing a perpetual flow of goods for sale and setting the staff on each morning to the most required tasks that my job was relatively easy. It was not long before I was dashing off to town each morning delivering plants, flowers and vegetables and then collecting timber, seeds, plant pots, insecticides and other necessities to bring back. I really loved the life and felt healthy, strong and very proud to see everything running so smoothly and productively.

The crowning triumph was to receive a call from the New Stanley Hotel asking if we could supply them with fruit and vegetables. When I delivered the first 200 lettuces, 200 cauliflowers and 300 mandarins, I was taken on a tour of the hotel kitchens and saw at first hand how food was processed, prepared and cooked to grace the tables of this internationally famous place. Just fancy, Bing Crosby, Stewart

Granger, James Stewart, Robert Mitchum and many other famous people who visited Kenya eating my produce. It was quite a thrill!

For security we bought an Alsatian bitch and named her Lassie, plus a Rhodesian ridgeback named Paddy; they were a delight to us, loyal and affectionate. Paddy was the real watch dog. How he guarded our home and us during our days at Mitini. The girls begged for rabbits and guinea pigs, so we made a large run and Omalanyo built houses for them. We also thought of poultry and soon had a good number of laying pullets to provide us with fresh eggs for breakfast.

Meanwhile, Johan's wife, Mary, continued to stay at the quarters. She was doomed to have tragic experiences. I had been to town one morning and, on return, just before lunch, I drove the van round the end of the house. Before I could stop I found that I was driving over large pieces of broken milk bottle glass. I jumped out and exploded angrily,

"Who on earth has thrown all that glass here. Come out here, all of you!"

There was no movement, no reply. I dashed into the house to find it silent and ghostly. No cleaned rooms, no food cooking on the stove, no table laid for lunch.

"Oh what has happened," I thought, "not Mau Mau, God. Please, not Mau Mau."

I was frightened as I slowly stepped outside again. As I did so I heard a groan from the back garden. Timidly I peeped round the back of the house to see Jotham, one of our gardeners, propped against the wall. He was sitting holding his left arm; blood was everywhere.

"Oh my goodness Jotham, what is it? What has happened?"

I ran over to find that he had been slashed through the arm at the elbow. He moaned with self-pity; I could not understand what he was trying to say; he was almost unconscious. I quickly went for towels, made a large pad and managed to stop the flow of blood. I shouted for help but no one came. Where were all the staff? What had happened?

A feeling of terror assailed me; had everyone been killed or injured? What could I do? He should be taken to hospital but I could not move him alone.

"Thank God", I whispered, as I heard Peter's car bringing him and the girls home for lunch. We all set to work; Peter, with Maureen to help him, got Jotham off to hospital. Left with the other two girls I decided to visit the quarters where, much to my surprise, I found the whole staff had shut themselves inside. After much coaxing and threatening I finally got Teresina to come out and speak to me.

"Now what is it? What has happened? You must tell me. Why are you all hiding in there?"

She was loath to speak. Gradually the others appeared and when they heard that Jotham was not dead, but had gone to hospital with the bwana, they opened up.

Mary, who was a pretty little thing, had apparently been amusing herself when Johan was at work by walking round the vegetable gardens to have little chats with the garden boys and the casual labour girls we took on for weeding. Unfortunately, for her and him, on this particular morning her chat had been with Jotham, when Johan appeared to collect the vegetables for lunch. He had not been married long and went berserk with rage and jealousy when he saw his wife talking to this big, handsome man. He had grabbed her and given her a tremendous hiding, whereupon Jotham came to her rescue saying she had done no harm. Johan would have none of this. He snatched a panga and let fly at his wife and Jotham. Mary ran off into the forest with Johan following, after delivering one last crippling slash at Jotham's arm. Jotham had collapsed and all the staff thinking he was dead had run away to lock themselves in the quarters. Teresina and Andrea joined them as they feared what the outcome would be.

I sternly told them what a lot of cowards they had been and why had they not helped Jotham instead of leaving him there. He would have died if he had not crawled back to the house where I found him.

"Now get back to work at once," I ordered them, "and you Teresina and Andrea go to the house and get some lunch ready immediately."

I also told three of the men to go in the forest to look for Johan and Mary and bring them back to me. Their eyes rolled with fright at the thought of this for they knew that members of the Mau Mau might be hiding in there. Nevertheless they went!

Peter and Maureen returned to say Jotham would be alright and we gradually got some semblance of order in the house. Around 4pm, as I sat down for a rest, I heard someone sobbing on the verandah. Mary stumbled into the room. She was a pitiful, sorry sight. There were large swellings and cuts on her face and body; her clothing was torn to shreds. She collapsed on the floor wailing and saying,

"Please take me to the bus. I want to go home to my parents. I don't want Johan to find me."

She was obviously terrified of him. What drama this is, I thought. I dressed her wounds and comforted her, letting her stay in the house until the matter could be sorted out. How primitive they can become, and how totally unaware of their behaviour and responsibilities in such moments I realised as I went to look for Johan. No apologies; he was unbendingly firm that what he had done was right and that he did not want such a wife. She must go to her parents and he too would go to get back his dowry. He never mentioned Jotham. One would hardly believe that he did not care whether the man was alive or dead! Jotham recovered and returned to work and the matter was forgotten by the Africans but certainly not by us!

The days flew by. There was so much to do and see to. Miss Carberry visited us and we tried to persuade her to either move into town or at least have someone to live in with her when we heard of more Mau Mau activities.

"No, never," she said, "I am fine. I am not afraid."

Nevertheless she agreed on an arrangement that if her phone was ever cut or she was in any trouble, she would fire her gun three times from an open window so that we would know of the danger.

We met our neighbours. One family, the Johnstones, had three children who visited us regularly. They became very friendly with the girls. As they had ponies, Val and Elaine wanted to ride too, so Phil-Phil and Aladdin, the white ponies were added to our menagerie. The girls were only allowed to ride inside our own boundary or just up and down to the Johnstones and they stuck to this religiously until one night as darkness fell, I suddenly became aware that Elaine was not in the house. Val had not ridden that day owing to homework, but Elaine had gone off with Caroline Johnstone.

"Don't worry Mum," said Val, "she'll be in the stables I'm sure."

But she was not and neither was Phil-Phil. The syce was there waiting with a lantern, also looking worried. These were the times one always had to acknowledge the danger in Kenya.

Where could they be? I rang the Johnstones. No they were not there. Alarmed by now, we gathered neighbours and garden boys to search the country lanes and forest tracks. Cars scoured the countryside; lights from lanterns flickered through the branches of the forest trees. We all shouted and hollered, our echoes ringing back across the valley, but there was no human reply. The cars all came back to check. Vivid imaginations played havoc with us. We were on the point of ringing the police, when in the distance we could hear the clip clop of horses' hooves. Gradually two little forms astride two small ponies took shape, emerging from the shrubbery bordering our neighbours property. The relief of seeing two scared little faces in the lamplight stopped our natural reaction to rebuke them. Where had they been? Were they alright? Were the horses alright? They were scared, but not of any danger, only of the dark. It appeared they had decided to venture next door and do a circular tour not realising the time. It got dark and they got lost, but:

"Why are you worried? Of course we would have got home alright."

Next day they were forbidden to ride again if they did not stay within the boundaries! They were only seven years old at the time.

Often at this time, we would wake in the mornings to find Army and Police surrounding our home. Paddy Murphy was usually there to explain that they had done a sweep through the forest. Attacks on people in the Nairobi area were becoming more frequent. Two young schoolboys had been killed when they were out with their air rifles. The Mau Mau had mistaken them for real guns and killed the boys to confiscate the guns. One day, Paddy told us they had caught the gang who killed the boys in our forest. Two other gangs were also rounded up. Another time, I drove home from my morning trip to town to find Paddy at the house. He asked me if I had a gun.

"No," I replied, "only Peter."

"Well, don't be scared, but we are surrounding the forest at the moment as we know two very dangerous men are in there. We want to drive them out on this side for easier capture. Stay in the house as they are desperate and lock all the doors."

I went inside taking the dogs with me and told my staff to stay in their quarters, but on reflection, once he had gone, I thought discretion the better part of valour, ran out to my van and drove back into town where I waited until lunch time to return with the family! Luckily we were told the men had been captured and all was well when we got back. Truly, the terrors of Mau Mau affected all life.

Paddy, the ridgeback, always followed me everywhere in the grounds, and if a garden boy or any African came too near me he would pounce on them immediately. Luckily he always came off at my command. One day I was picking grapefruit from a tree in the orchard when a neighbour came round the other side of the tree. He would have been dead but for Paddy's obedience to my call. Another time, a new garden boy was following me round the back verandah where I was about to show him where to put chopped wood for the boiler fires. All I heard was a choking sound; I turned to see the boy pinned to the wall by this great golden dog, for all the world like a lion on the kill. He had already bitten the boy twice in the arms and was about to go for his throat. I was petrified but managed to shout and Paddy, as usual, came away at my command. The poor boy almost dead with fright, staggered into the bathroom with me. I sat him on a stool whereupon he immediately fell over backwards in a dead faint. So once again we had a hurried trip to hospital.

Once Paddy accepted newcomers and staff he never bothered them unless they came too near members of the family but then it was a different matter. To us, he was always loving and affectionate, always ready for a game or a little showing off. One morning he came leaping along the verandah and dropped something at my feet, his tail wagging with glee.

"Oh no, he's killed one of the children from the quarters!" I yelled, for there was a little black hand with torn flesh and bone attached to it. I couldn't bear to look again. Peter came out and said:

"Alright dear, now steady on there," and then, "No, no, it's not a toto (child), I think it's a Colobus monkey hand."

And so it was. We had a few of them in the forest and Paddy could not stand the sight or sound of them, so this one had come to a sorry end.

CHAPTER NINE

"SACUNDA"

Staff for the house became a problem as Teresina, Johan and Andrea were unable to cope with everything, and Johan had certainly become a question mark after the slashing affair. One day I was told there was a man outside asking for work. It was not recommended to take on strangers or people not introduced or vouched for by previous employers in those days of Mau Mau. I looked out and saw an old, thin, wiry man with bowed legs and a small, wrinkled but humorous face. Silently he handed me his registration card and references.

I was surprised to see he was of the Machaga tribe of Tanganyika who reside on the slopes of Mt. Kilimanjaro. His references revealed that he had worked for several notable people including a previous Governor of Kenya. Were they faked? What was he doing unemployed? How old was he? He told me he had left his last post to go home for several months. Now he was back looking for work. He did not tell me that he was 71 and had been retired! After ringing one or two previous employers and being told that he was a very good man, I decided to take him on trial for a week. Sacunda, for that was his name, stayed with us for years, and was still insisting at 84 that he was capable of carrying on.

How could he ever be forgotten? As soon as he entered the house he became the perfect major-domo. His air of authority as soon as he donned kanzu, fez and waistcoat, his supreme efficiency at running a large establishment, his control over other staff, were something to behold. He never missed a trick. He was totally committed to us; we were his family and he respected and cared for us and our possessions; they were his. The house glistened with cleanliness; floors, silver and brass shone, linen was snow white, starched and perfect. Visitors were greeted with respect. If we were out and he knew they were friends, he would serve them with tea or drinks until we returned. Baths were run for Peter and me, clothes laid out in the evening, even cuff links and jewellery. Slippers were always ready when we came home tired. He bullied Teresina to do the same for the girls. She was a large, jolly, good natured girl inclined to be lazy and many a time she received the length of Sacunda's tongue, berating her for idleness and slovenly work. Poor Teresina!

I asked him who taught him to work so well and he said the German Police Commissioner's wife in Dar-es-Salaam when he was a young boy of 14. She had trained him to perfection. He said he had cried himself to sleep many a night because she had made him do a thing over and over again until it was right. For example, starching and ironing a white damask tablecloth 25 times until she was satisfied with it. He bore her no resentment and said that her efforts had resulted in him being able to obtain good employment all his life and that he admired her. To appreciate this, one had to imagine a small African boy who had lived all his years in a mud hut, brought up close to nature with no domestic trimmings, who had never even seen a damask tablecloth or a silver dish, let alone know how to care for them. Yes, one could admire her, watching the finished product.

He was certainly a great support for us, especially as I was so involved in dealing with the market garden business. He made sure the duties in the house were all carried out to perfection and that healthy meals were prepared by the cook. Many of our friends became quite envious when comparing him with their own staff, and I suspected that one or two of them had tried to lure him away, but thankfully he remained loyal to us.

Johnnie and Doreen eventually left us to move into their own home. I think Doreen was pleased to move as some of the episodes had scared her and she said she felt safer in the city. So, Dermott Kydd, a friend, asked if he could come and stay with us. He was a bachelor who had come out for the Lands Department to do a survey of all the Kenya farms. I read only the other day that he had been awarded the OBE for his invaluable work for the British and Kenyan Governments during his 25 years service.

I had noticed for some time that young African men were appearing, singly, in the afternoons; smart and well dressed. They would walk up the long driveway and disappear round the far end of the house on their way to our quarters. We inquired who they were visiting and were told they were Teresina's brothers. As she was off duty in the afternoons, we hesitated to interfere until one day I heard loud yells and screams from her house. I looked out to see a man carrying away a gramophone and records with Teresina chasing him demanding their return, also her watch, etc., etc. The outcome of this was that Teresina had to go. Her "brothers" were paying for her favours and she had fallen out with this one. I discussed the affair with Sacunda and he suggested that both she and Johan should leave and he would find two good men to replace them. He said we did not really need an ayah now for the girls were growing up. Johan showed no emotion at his dismissal, but Teresina cried and said she would be good if only she could stay. She was a kind, good hearted girl, always cheerful and laughing, but prostitution on the premises was hardly to be encouraged, so firmly I said she must leave. She had been good to the girls and they would miss her, but so be it.

The two replacements were good at their work, one especially, a very happy soul, who smiled perpetually. Andrea was growing up, he was very young when he came to us, but now he was responsible and efficient under Sacunda's tuition and took pride in his many duties. His only aversion was to polishing the huge verandah at the front of the house. I was amused one day when I accidentally came across him doing this chore to find him throwing a door mat the length of the verandah and muttering how he hated this. I heartily agreed, it was a lousy job, but crept away before he could see me, or he would have been very embarrassed.

One morning I caught a glimpse of a European walking up the long drive to the house. As he approached, I thought:

"Oh my goodness! It can't be. Not so soon, surely not so soon. It can't be Mr. Mitchell."

But it was. It really was. I could only think,

"Oh dear, we've got settled in so well and now he's come back and will want his house."

I went to meet him. He was as usual charming and easy to talk to. I took him inside where we had a long chat during which he told me that he had not been able to settle in England,

"You know, you said I would come back one day, but I never

dreamed it would be so soon," he said, "but I was miserable after the first few weeks and I missed all my friends."

He assured me that he did not wish to come back to live in Mitini, which made me very happy, but that he was buying a piece of land from one of our neighbours where he was to build a small house. When it was ready, he came and collected his belongings and was soon organised and happy. We visited him many times as he was a wonderfully hospitable man. In time, he married again and we were very pleased for him.

We realised some time later that we had not as yet had a holiday, so we decided we should arrange for one at the Coast. Dermott promptly offered to run the business and take care of everything for us, so there was nothing to stop us going ahead with a visit to Mombasa.

CHAPTER TEN

COAST HOLIDAY

Today Kenya has many large impersonal luxury hotels spread along her coastline to cater for the thousands of tourists who visit there regularly. When we made our first journey to her beautiful beaches, there were perhaps not more than six small family hotels, usually thatched roof, with open banda style dining rooms where the meals provided were the main consideration and luxury was of little consequence, though every homely comfort was provided. They were wonderfully free and easy places, full of character, where people relaxed, laughed, joked, made lifelong friends round the cosy bars in the evenings and returned up-country feeling unbelievably refreshed. On our first holiday, we did not stay at one of these as we had been loaned a beach cottage at Kikambala, but we visited them for odd meals and drinks. In later years, we stayed at them all in turn.

We knew that we would have to take food and bed linen with us and one of the servants to help with the chores, so there was quite a packing up to cater for a family of six for two weeks. The station wagon was so laden we only just managed to squeeze in as we waved to Dermott and set off on a 320 mile journey on a dirt road.

We were in a happy, carefree, holiday mood as we chattered and sang for the first fifty miles or so. We had passed the town of Athi River and seen our giraffes still nibbling at the thorn trees, and then the Ulu Hills, a picturesque landmark, carefully winding our way over these and then down again to flat country round Sultan Hamud, which was our first stop for a much required drink at an Indian duka (store). The Indians were always pleased to greet travellers and have a friendly chat, for they must have felt isolated and lonely at times as there was not a great deal of traffic at that time. Sultan Hamud was not a pretty place with its dusty main street and tin shacks. The railway station provided the only other interest of the day when the one up/one down passenger trains from Kampala to Mombasa passed through, plus a few goods trains. Shy children peeped round doors, giggling as we smiled at them. A few Masai strolled, or just stood in the streets.

Dogs lay in the dust snapping at the flies.

We travelled on towards distant hills which meant more curves and rocky surfaces, also drifts where water poured across the road in wet weather. Luckily they were dry this time, but we had other experiences on future journeys when we once had to sit in the car all night until the water subsided.

We had seen giraffe and zebra at Athi River, and now as we approached Kibwezi through a green, well wooded area, due to the proximity of a river, notice boards attached to trees warned us to beware of elephants crossing. We didn't see elephants, but we did see dozens of baboons and monkeys swinging in the trees and ambling on the verge of the road, screaming and chattering at us. Seen in large numbers like that they are a little frightening and overpowering. One baboon jumped on the bonnet of the car, leering in at us, but decided not to prolong his visit as the car lurched over the uneven surface of the road.

Kibwezi was a cluster of Indian dukas, more attractive in the shade of the trees. We only made a short halt, as we wished to reach the halfway mark at Mtito Andei by lunch time, and very glad we were when we saw the old Mac's Inn come into view. The heat of noon was having a wearying effect and we needed to stretch our legs and freshen up. Mac's Inn was a solitary haven in the midst of the more tedious part of our journey - the flat country of red sand, thorn trees and scrub which leads down to the Teita Hills and Voi. We had a pleasant meal there, served by attentive African waiters, and a chat with the landlord. These people who spent their working lives in isolated places with no modern labour-saving aids, always managed to produce a variety of appetising dishes and cool drinks. They also provided an atmosphere never recaptured. The dining rooms were spotlessly clean, shady and cool, decorated with local bric-a-brac; pleasant chatter and jokes were the order of the day. A sincere desire to please their customers and a genuine interest in them as fellow human beings, ensured further visits as often as possible.

On we went, down the dusty road, and soon we had the thrilling experience of seeing our first elephants crossing the thoroughfare just ahead of us. We pulled up at a safe distance to watch four of them casually making their way over. Out came the cameras, we had to wait quite a long time before they slowly disappeared into the nearby shrubbery. Although an African, Andrea had never seen an elephant as he came from a district where they were not prevalent, so, if anything, he was more excited than we were. Further along we saw others in the bush, usually congregated around baobab trees. Of course, they are very destructive in this regard, most of the trees being torn to shreds or left mere stumps.

Way ahead we could just discern the Teita Hills. Now we were approaching one of the large camps where members of Mau Mau were imprisoned. Armed guards were visible in the control towers as we drove by. It was a depressing sight which took some time to overcome.

Voi was larger than the other places, quite a busy little town, with a main thoroughfare, an hotel, more substantial shops and business areas as it is the centre for the local farms and sisal estates. Between Voi and Mombasa we had brief relief on a stretch of tar sealed road called McKinnon Road, an area which had been a military base during World War Two.

Again, we felt weary for this journey with its combination of heat, dust and cramped seating was taking its toll. When we reached the summit of Mariakani, twenty miles or so from Mombasa and saw palm trees gently swaying in the breeze, it was a blessed tonic. From then on we were so busy absorbing the new surroundings we forgot all the discomfort. There ahead was the sea glistening in the sunshine, there across a causeway were all the ships in the harbour, cargo and passenger, there were the mixed inhabitants, African, Arab and Indian. In the shade of palms, small mosques and coastal type homes with thatched roofs lined the outskirts of town along with the inevitable Indian dukas. We had to find our way to Nyali Toll Bridge which had been built to connect the island of Mombasa to the northern coastline of Kenya, for Kikambala, our destination, was seventeen miles north. As we crossed the bridge, the old harbour of Mombasa was on our right, a mass of small vessels and romantic Arab dhows, banked by buildings of Arabic and Asian design. They looked like some Arabian fairy tale picture in the soft becoming light of early evening.

The road now took us through coastal villages, winding its way amongst shrubbery and palms. The Moslems were offering their evening prayers at small mosques; womenfolk and children surrounded wells collecting their water ration for the night. Goats leaped through the bush at our approach, their bells tinkling in the evening air. We pressed on, anxious to find our cottage before darkness fell. Suddenly we descended a steep hill at the foot of which flowed the waters of Mtwapa Creek. We had to wait in line to be taken across by ferry, this being just a large raft. A fitting climax to our journey was being gently pulled away from the shore, as the attendants sang to us, making up their own words of how the bwana and his wife were taking their children on a long safari for a lovely holiday at the seaside. They blew in conch shells, laughed and joked with the children and safely deposited us on the other side. Soon after this pleasant interlude we found the lane to our cottage. Looking back, the setting sun had turned everything into a gold and orange world relieved by black silhouette palms.

Our beach house was an attractive, thatched roofed abode with a large verandah, surrounded by colourful shrubs and palm trees. Only twenty yards away the ripples of the ocean gently lapped on the white beach and in the distance we could hear the stronger waves pounding on the reef.

We stretched our aching limbs, unpacked the station wagon, explored the house and now it was dark we lit the Tilley lamps and made up the beds. We found only an old oil cooker, so decided to have boiled eggs and call it a day. The toilet, we found, was far in the bush down a little path bordered by dense undergrowth. Visions of snakes and spiders made each visit a combined operation, with someone carrying a lamp, the others armed with big sticks. Soon the girls were all asleep and Andrea settled in his quarters. Peter and I relaxed on the verandah with a drink, breathing in the refreshing sea air. It was so beautiful, so peaceful, so far from the cares of the world. A gentle breeze rustled the palm leaves and to perfect it all, a full moon appeared.

In the early hours, an agitated shouting awoke us from a deep sleep. We jumped up and found Andrea frantically rushing up and down the verandah shouting,

"Come quickly, memsahib, bwana, watoto, come quickly, we will all be killed. Hurry, hurry! See the water is getting very close."

The noise of the incoming tide had aroused him and he was genuinely terrified, for he had never seen the sea before and knew nothing of tides ebbing and flowing. I'm afraid we laughed as we tried to explain that the water would stop at a cèrtain point, then turn and go away again. He was not convinced and begged us to at least put all our things in the car ready to leave. Peter tried to impart further knowledge, but we still found Andrea at dawn sitting on the verandah watching the water. His look of wonder at lunch-time when the waves receded beyond the reef is still etched on my memory, as is his proud relating of information on oceans, tides and reefs to his fellow workers on our return home.

By the critical light of day, we found our cottage, to say the least, hardly hygienically clean, but holidaymakers are not usually interested in household chores. Peter's advice was to let sleeping dogs lie and not stir up germs by giving the place a spring clean! Outdoors the beautiful white beach beckoned; we swam each day as soon as the tide came in, in water that was soft and gentle and always at the right temperature. The girls lived in their bathing suits. Trips to the reef were made at low tide when they collected shells and examined the marine life in all the small pools. Sand crabs were a great fascination, scuttling around on the beach and disappearing into their holes when disturbed. Each evening, when a cool, refreshing breeze arose, we took a long walk along the beach, passing all the other holiday houses. On these walks we would see the girls of the Giriama tribe, dressed only in grass skirts, gracefully carrying an earthenware jar, presumably of water, on their heads. They were making their way homewards along the sandy tracks through the bush at the rear of the beach. We would call at the only hotel for a drink and a chat with other holidaymakers, and so back to our cottage for the evening meal and bed.

We ate very well as Africans called at the house daily, selling us fruit, vegetables, freshly caught fish and shellfish. They would stay and cook lobsters for us, climb the palm trees and throw down the coconuts from which we obtained refreshing drinks.

After a week of lazing, we decided to spend a day visiting Mombasa. The town is on the sheltered island which we found much hotter than the breezy mainland. Walking around was quite exhausting in the humid atmosphere. The shopping area was, as usual, Indian dukas, where a fantastic collection of curios was available. An open meat and vegetable market let off a pungent aroma as did a fish market down a side street. There were many picturesque mosques. Arabic buildings lined streets leading down to the old harbour. Here one could watch craftsmen in open shops making attractively designed jewellery from gold, silver and copper. Arab dhows had pulled into berths in the old harbour, some of them unloading exciting cargoes of Persian rugs, old coffee pots and Arab chests amongst many other items, all exceedingly tempting. If one bargained with the Arab captain, it was possible to obtain a Persian rug or an Arab brass studded chest for £50 in those days. These, of course, were a satisfying possession in any home.

We drove around the outer areas near the main harbour where lovely homes had been built to catch the sea breeze, amongst them Government House. Here too, we saw avenues of baobab trees under which we rested to watch the ships sailing in and out of the harbour. The ferry boats, taking vehicles and passengers to the south mainland, were tossed around like cockleshells in the wash from these larger vessels, which made us happy that we were staying on the north side where we only had to cross a bridge. Mombasa Club in its delightful setting by the water tempted us to stay for lunch. These old clubs in every town had a reciprocal arrangement for membership which entitled one to use their services when travelling away from home. They were usually very comfortable with excellent service and good food, a real home from home.

Rested and replete, we now crossed the road to Fort Jesus, the highlight of our day's outing. Here we knew was the history of Mombasa. Vasco da Gama recorded that:

"Here he had found a large city seated upon an eminence washed by the sea, and by the sea a low lying fortress."

This fortress, however, was not Fort Jesus for it was not built until later. The Portuguese took over Mombasa in the 1500's but had a restless 200 years or so of attacks and reprisals. The Turks drove out the Portuguese for four years in 1585 and it was after this that Fort Jesus was built. An inscription over the door commemorates the completion date in 1595.

In 1631 the Arabs captured the fort from the Portuguese and held it until 1699 when the Portuguese returned, but not for long. Three years later the whole garrison of 3,000 men except for eleven survivors was massacred by the Arabs who now kept control, rather shakily, until 1784, but after that they had full and final control over Mombasa and the island of Zanzibar.

In the 1800's Mombasa was offered to the British, but it was not until 1877 when the Sultan of Zanzibar granted the British East Africa Association a concession for a period of 50 years, with the right to collect taxes and administer justice and government, that the offer was accepted.

As we stepped inside, we could feel the pages of history unfolding. Although part of the Fort is an excellent museum, other areas have been preserved in their original state and, as we climbed the stone steps to the parapets and explored the living quarters where bougainvillaea trailed over a trellis, I closed my eyes and had the eerie feeling of ghosts of former occupants still very much in possession.

Another day we drove north to visit Malindi and on the way stopped off to explore the ancient city of Gedi, which proved just as interesting. Gedi was discovered buried in the bush in the 1920's. The local inhabitants were afraid to visit it for they said it was haunted. Mr. Kirkman who set up the museum in Fort Jesus was put in charge of excavations which uncovered streets, shops, houses, mosques and the fact that it had been a flourishing and mainly Arab city in the 12th and 13th centuries. Also, that there had been a much more ancient city, possibly Persian. Many relics were unearthed including a great deal of Chinese pottery. It appeared to have been a walled city with large gateways. After looking around, I felt a little like the local people and would not have wished to visit it after dark.

Malindi, 76 miles north of Mombasa, was even then very popular with holidaymakers; there were larger, smarter hotels on the foreshore than the smaller ones down the coast. Surfing was possible in the rougher seas and the beaches were immensely wide. The Sindbad Hotel, of Arabic design, with arches and whitewashed walls was where we made a break for lunch. We met many Arab inhabitants here emerging from their small white homes, which gave the town a more North African atmosphere.

Vasco da Gama was made welcome by the people of Malindi in 1498 before he sailed on to India. In 1960 a monument to him was unveiled there by Dr. Pedro Pereira of Portugal. This is in the form of a 20 foot pillar adorned with the Cross of the Order of Christ which rises from a mosaic pool. We visited this and then returned down the coast road to our cosy cottage, which we did not leave again until the holiday was over. These trips we had found rather tiring in the coastal heat and humidity and we were quite satisfied with the ones we had made on our first holiday in this fascinating and totally different environment.

Our last few days flew by, blissfully peaceful except for the short visit of a brightly coloured snake which wriggled quickly across the garden and disappeared abruptly into the bush, and the sight one morning of a black widow spider busily weaving a huge web between two pillars of the verandah. Peter speedily managed to persuade her to move to another district, but not without some element of danger.

As we climbed the hill out of Mombasa on our way back to Nairobi and looked back at the disappearing coastline, an indescribable yearning to stay with the kind of life we had just experienced assailed us all. We were to find this same feeling creep over us at the same place on all subsequent visits to the coast.

CHAPTER ELEVEN

FURTHER DAYS AT MITINI

As we drove up to our home after the long tiring trip from Mombasa, we could see the police landrover of Paddy Murphy standing in the drive. We felt a moment of anxiety which was dispelled at the sight of Dermott and all our staff obviously safe and happy. Paddy waited patiently in his vehicle until we got over all the greetings and arranged for the children to be fed and prepared for bed. Then he came in for a drink with Peter, Dermott and I. Apologising for disturbing us at such a time he quickly got to the point, producing a pair of gardening gloves and asking if we recognised them.

"Oh yes," I said, "those are my gloves which I leave in one of the gardening sheds."

"Well," he replied, "last night we found these when we were digging up an enormous quantity of articles from under the floor of an African hut not far from here. We were really searching for guns." He went on, "Will you come to the landrover and see if anything else belongs to you."

We found that most of the contents were from our stores; rolls of chicken wire, tools, timber, tarpaulins and other things.

"I'm sorry about this," Paddy now said, "but I must question all your staff to see if I can find out who, amongst them, aided and abetted this theft, as it is obvious there must have been inside help."

Off he went to the quarters, eventually returning with a downcast Jotham, the African I had found slashed by Johan. We were amazed as he had been a hard working servant, always polite and cheerful, and apparently happy in his job. However, Paddy had found out, without question, that he was the culprit.

The outcome of this was that I had to go to court a short time later to identify the goods, and to hear Jotham sentenced, along with his friends, to six months in jail. I felt upset and confused by his unpredictable action and realised I had a lot to learn about life with the natives.

We had not been back long from our holiday when our eldest daughter, Maureen, came home one day to say that the school she attended was being moved to Eldoret and that she could either go there as a boarder, or transfer to another school in Nairobi. Naturally we were disturbed and thought it best for her to stay in Nairobi. Eldoret was two hundred miles north and, although not in a Mau Mau area, we were not in favour of her being so far away. However, she later discovered that all her best friends and all of the teachers were going to Eldoret. After much pleading on her part, we gave in, not without a few misgivings, and consented to her joining them. She was to spend two years there which she thoroughly enjoyed; the clear fresh air and regular routine kept her fit and full of high spirits. I'm sure she has many cherished memories of her time at the Highlands School.

Her initiation, however, was a little traumatic. Peter and I took her to Eldoret by car one weekend for the start of the first term. After a great deal of fuss by Sacunda, who had helped to pack all the clothes and gear she would require, we left early on the Saturday morning. It was the rainy season, but luckily, Saturday was a dry day.

We had not travelled further than Nakuru before, one hundred miles to the west. This was a beautiful ride up through the coffee growing area of Limuru and then down the side of the Rift Valley to the little church in the valley. The view, on this day, however, was dimmed by rain clouds, but we could still see Mount Longonot and decided we must try to climb it sometime. On we went to Naivasha for a quick coffee at the small hotel, followed by a brief visit to the lake of the same name which is a mile or two from town.

This lake and its surrounds have been the backdrop for many films, such as 'Mr. Moses', in which Robert Mitchum starred. Hell's Gate is nearby, the entrance to a thermal valley, a very modest version of Rotorua in New Zealand. We had no time to linger, but we stole a few minutes by the lake edge to watch the prolific bird life. Umbrella thorn trees surround the lake; hidden by them are many pioneer homes, mostly wooden with large verandahs, all surrounded by attractive lawns and gardens. Joy Adamson, of 'Born Free' fame, was to have a house here in years to come, also Joan and Alan Root, the well-known wildlife film couple, whom we eventually knew well, and with whom Maureen would one day work, but we knew nothing of this on that day.

On we sped to Nakuru, passing Elmenteita where Lord Delamere, the early pioneer, had settled. Lake Elmenteita was a carpet of pink flamingos making us gasp with admiration as something disturbed them and they took to the air like a huge fleet of small pink and white aircraft. What a thrill! Wildlife conservationists spend a great deal of time in this area, at and around Nakuru, where Lake Nakuru is so famous for all the species of water birds. I'm sure nowadays they do all in their power to protect this fantastic collection of the world's wildlife which cannot be surpassed elsewhere.

We called at the Stag's Head Hotel in Nakuru, an attractive little market town, the centre for the local farmers. Africans seated on the footpath outside were offering for sale the usual wood carvings and Kisii soapstone vases and candlesticks. They had learned to barter almost as well as the Indians, so one usually came away with a souvenir.

Moving along we ascended the hill out of Nakuru, looking back at the lake and the Meningai crater. By the lake are smaller hills, one resembling a resting lion, hence its name, Lion Hill. We passed the Farm Hotel, a pleasing stop on future safaris, which provided excellent accommodation and meals. Large tracts of wheat appeared as we reached Mau Summit, and later forests which had been planted by the government. The road from Nakuru was a dirt one, so we were thankful it was still a dry day. We were later to reach an altitude of 9000 ft. at the minute town of Equator which is really just a railway station and the odd store. Here we saw a board informing us that we were now crossing the equator. This was wild, rolling country, with more forests and dairy farms appearing here and there. Timberoa followed with its well-known hill descending to the flat plateau country of Eldoret where the altitude fell to 6000 ft. The air was sharp and bracing, a little chilly at this time of the year. Pine and wattle trees lined the road as we drove into town, another farming centre where quite large stores catered for the mechanical and other needs of the local population.

We made our way to the new school, where we met the Headmistress, other teachers, and house mistresses; one of these escorted us to Maureen's dormitory. By now, it was very cold and heavy rain had set in. To my horror, I discovered that the dormitory had no glass in the windows. The rain was pouring in onto beds, cupboards and floor. Mud was everywhere. The mistress explained that the workmen had been unable to meet the deadline, but that the glass would be put in the following week. Although the school was an impressive building, I could not help feeling worried for Maureen's welfare in this cheerless room. Catching sight of some of her mates, she now dashed away, happy and excited. On return, she said,

"Oh Mummy don't worry so, I'm sure we will be alright, they will put up some shutters for the night or something."

That night, as we listened to the heavy rain rattling on the tin roof of the old hotel where we stayed, I could not help wishing Maureen had spent the night with us. Next morning, as we drove to the school, prior to leaving for Nairobi, Peter consoled me saying,

"Look, she'll be okay I'm sure. Stop being an old hen. It's all a big adventure for her you know, and she has got the support of all her friends. You'll see when we get there."

However, when we saw Maureen after a wet, cold night, with perhaps a share of homesickness thrown in, her little face was not the confident one of the night before. She put on a show of brightness for our sakes, telling us that her best friend had the bed next to her, and how they had got up early for a nice warm bath and that they were really fine.

"Don't you worry, we'll soon have the windows in," she assured us (and herself too I thought!). As we drove away, her bottom lip trembled, but she bravely held back the tears.

It is hard for a parent to part with a child one has cared for and protected for so many years, so I was feeling upset, and I'm sure Peter was too. When I am upset I always talk a lot to try and cover up my emotional state, so I started a long tirade on the good and bad aspects of living in, and being educated at, a boarding school. Receiving no response from Peter I suddenly realised that the effect of the heavy rain we were now experiencing was taking all his concentration driving on the resultant wet, skiddy road.

The rain continued to fall so heavily that at times it was difficult to see through the windscreen at all. I suggested that perhaps we should return to Eldoret and wait for better weather. I had not forgotten the hazard of climbing 3000ft at Timberoa, where I knew many people had suffered hair-raising experiences in the heavy rains.

"No," said Peter, "I must get on. I have to be in the office tomorrow without fail. Don't worry, we'll get through."

I had a very stubborn husband when duty called, so forced myself to keep quiet.

My fears were realised as we came to the dreaded hill, for there was the unbelievable sight of lorries, buses and private cars, at least thirty of them, looking as if some gigantic landslide had thrown them around like toys. Some were in ditches on both sides of the road, some broadside across the road and some just stuck in a foot or so of thick mud. What a mess.

Of course we could not go on and the weather was now devilish. Peter struggled out in it to talk to other drivers. Any outside help was not hopeful in this isolated, sparsely populated area, but some of them had gone off to the nearest farms to see if they could borrow tractors. The result was a long wait all day, and a night in the car! We had only drinks, biscuits and sweets with us. What a strain it was with no sign of a break in the rain. The piercing cold numbed our bodies and brains; we could only doze fitfully during the hours of darkness which I thought would never end. Next morning, how thankful we were to find the rain had eased off. The tractors arrived and we gradually got out of the predicament. I closed my eyes and prayed when our turn came to climb the hill as there was a very steep drop on one side and it was so easy to stick or slide in the mud. However, we made it safely and continued on our way still feeling somewhat shattered.

Experiences such as this were common occurrences in the rainy season, as most of the dirt roads were in atrocious condition. In later years this one was tar sealed, not before time for the people who lived in that district. So, we always remembered Maureen's first days at boarding school. We also arranged for her to travel to and fro by train on holidays in future wet weather.

I was thankful to be back at home safe and sound and once more settled into the usual routine. More blood curdling activities by the Mau Mau were reported. Paddy Murphy must have had a premonition that something was about to happen to Miss Carberry as he paid her several visits during which he begged her to move into town. She became nervous on a few occasions, firing her gun as we had arranged, but these turned out to be false alarms for quite some time. Then one night about 9pm we were roused by loud thumping, banging and shouting coming from the direction of her home. The three pistol shots followed.

"This is for real!" Peter and Dermott exclaimed at once.

They went out on the verandah armed with their guns. I rang the police post and three of our neighbours asking them to come round as quickly as possible. The shouts and bangings increased in volume and I turned cold. Peter and Dermott were half way to the cottage as the neighbours arrived and joined them. I shut myself inside with the children and the dogs, listening intently for the arrival of the police who were not long in coming. Now the bangings ceased and I could hear the sound of many men crashing through the forest undergrowth; guns were being fired, voices shouted instructions; I had never been so scared in my life. Suddenly there was a desperate yell that went on and on.

"Dear Lord," I whispered "that's a European voice. Who has got hurt?"

I froze as the agonising moments went by. It seemed an eternity until I heard footsteps and voices coming towards the house, Peter's voice being one of them. The relief was enormous as I dashed to open the door. Emerging from the darkness I could see two figures supporting a third one; Peter and Dermott were helping Johnnie Johnstone and I was afraid for him, thinking he had been shot. However, the men were laughing as they staggered up the verandah steps.

"Whatever is it?" I exploded. "Was that Johnnie yelling out?"

"Yes it was," Peter replied, "don't worry now, he'll be alright. He tripped up when we were chasing the Mau Mau and fell backwards over into that prickly cactus near our drive."

Poor Johnnie's face was a picture of agony!

"Come on Johnnie. Let's get you laid out so we can see the damage," Peter advised.

Our neighbours now arrived to say that the police were still following the Mau Mau through the forest.

We all had a strong drink and the men spent the next hour or two pulling out the prickly spines of cactus from Johnnie's back and lower parts with tweezers to the accompaniment of lots of 'Ooh's' and 'Aah's' from Johnnie, meanwhile giving me a running commentary on what had happened.

"But what about Miss Carberry?" I asked, "Is she alright?"

"Yes, she's with Paddy Murphy now. When we arrived the Mau Mau were still trying to batter their way into the houseboys' quarters and had not started on her cottage, luckily for her, as they really meant business tonight. There were a lot of them, but they all ran off when we disturbed them."

Poor Miss Carberry, she must have had a dreadful fright. She was taken care of by the police that night and arranged to move into town the very next day. She hated leaving her little cottage, but life is sweet, and she had been very fortunate to escape from harm.

Unfortunately, the culprits all got away that night, but luckily no real damage was done and we had many a good laugh later at Johnnie's expense.

CHAPTER TWELVE

FAREWELL MITINI

Things went on quietly at Mitini after the departure of Miss Carberry, when a young couple along with a male friend, rented the cottage.

The market garden prospered, so when friends suggested that I should grow mushrooms in some of the vacant sheds I thought why not, and decided to give it a try.

We had a good friend, Svend, a Dane, who had been managing a large sisal estate at Solai near Nakuru. He had a New Zealander wife named Atholl, who on completing her nursing training, had set off to travel the world. She had worked in Australia, South Africa, Rhodesia and then travelled on to Kenya. There she met Svend, and married him. Svend was a hard working man with a delightful sense of humour coupled with a desire to do well in life for his wife and family, for when we came to know him he had three children. Their homestead at Solai was in an isolated spot surrounded by hills. Svend knew that Mau Mau terrorists hid out in the hills and he was anxious as he feared they watched every movement of his wife and children. We visited them there one weekend when he told us that only a few days previously he and an African employee were going along a road through the sisal when suddenly a terrorist jumped out of the ditch at the roadside and advanced towards him with a raised panga. The African employee, who carried a bow and arrows, very quickly aimed an arrow at the terrorist and killed him. Many loyal, in this case non-Kikuyu, servants had great protective instincts for their white employers on lonely farms at that time.

As soon as he could raise the finance Svend took his family away from this dangerous spot to live at Naivasha where they had a small farm by the side of the lake. He kept cattle and later opened a butcher's shop and a delicatessen in the small town. To help with this he brought out two butchers from Denmark and very soon they were supplying goods to hotels in Nairobi and Mombasa and later to the catering establishment at Nairobi airport. He then went on to purchase a huge estate at the Kinangop, the area on the rim of the Rift Valley escarpment above Naivasha. It was the property of a relative of an English aristocratic family who was leaving Kenya because he already had decided that there was no future for farmers there. Svend grew quick cash crops and became very rich.

He joked that the reason for his success was that when he needed capital for further ventures he always drove to the bank in a Mercedes car and wore a new suit! Of course, it was much more than that; everyone knew him as a hard-working, trustworthy person, always reliable and helpful to others. His hospitality was well known and his wife Atholl was a gourmet cook. To be entertained by them was a great experience.

He visited our house on one of his trips to Nairobi when I told him of my interest in mushroom growing. Immediately, he said that I could have as much horse manure as I liked from his farm.

"Why don't you borrow a pick-up and come out one weekend?"

Peter managed to borrow one from his company so away we went one Sunday morning, accompanied by Dermott. Secretly, I think, we all wondered if we would be capable of returning with what we set out to collect, but being in holiday mood these thoughts seemed of no serious consequence. As we drove into the farmyard, Svend directed us to a large shed where two or three Africans were waiting. He told them to load the truck so that it would be ready when we wished to leave.

"There then, that's that!" he greeted us. "Now we can relax and have a good day. It's great to have you here."

I remembered other 'good' days with Svend - one when we all ended up at the small hotel in Naivasha where he danced on the bar, clad only in a grass skirt! Another one, when we prepared to leave, only to find that he was not in favour of this. As we tried to drive away, he jumped on the roof of the car, clung to the luggage rack and would not dismount. We drove him through Naivasha in this precarious position, much to the astonishment of the natives. Of course, we returned to appease him.

Their new home on the Kinangop was huge and had two guest wings of bedrooms and bathrooms which I am sure had accommodated many guests over the years. There were other areas of sitting rooms, billiard room, library, and even a bar with panelled walls. There were stools at the long bar and even pumps for the beer; a real replica of an old English pub.

Our girls joined the Gerstrom children and dashed off for an energetic day in the exciting environment of a farm. We were taken on a tour of the countryside followed by pre-lunch drinks which led the way to a magnificent feast prepared by Atholl. The usual shouts of "Skoal" along with the various courses left us in merry mood but also very reluctant to leave our comfortable chairs in the lounge after coffee. We spent the afternoon reminiscing, chatting on this and that and thoroughly enjoyed the change of a day out.

When the time came to leave Svend did not deter us as he took seriously the need to return safely to Nairobi with our heavy load. Threatening clouds over the lake warned of possible rain as we made our way to the pick-up. We found this well and truly loaded, not only was it full, but full to the level of the cab roof! Now came the problem of where we could all ride home. In the end, Peter took the girls in the cab with him and Dermott and I dug holes in the dry manure and sat down in these, hoping that we could hang on. Reaching these unappealing positions had its laughable moments as one can imagine.

"Don't drive too fast Peter." I begged.

Why had I not insisted in off-loading some of this cargo I thought miserably as we jerked away. I felt most insecure and also felt the chill of the evening air. Dermott and I wore shirts and trousers and found that we soon began to shiver as the cold air rushed by. This was soon followed by heavy rain. We had descended from the Kinangop into the Rift Valley and now we had to climb the escarpment on the way to Nairobi. When the rain arrived, Peter increased speed, no doubt thinking that he must get home quickly to relieve Dermott and I from our uncomfortable situation. However, this was something of a disaster for Dermott and I were now thrown around in a dangerous manner. We shouted, but unfortunately, Peter didn't hear or understand for quite some time. Luckily, he slowed down as we started up the escarpment as I had been having visions of us both being thrown to the floor of the Rift Valley. We dug deeper into our now wet manure. All went well until somewhere about five or six miles out of Nairobi when we heard a loud bang and the pick-up swerved and shuddered across the road in a frightening manner. Dermott grabbed me and shouted,

"Jump!"

He took me with him and we fell into the long, wet grass. Recovering my senses I was so thankful to see the pick-up still upright where it had come to a halt with the front end partly in a ditch ten yards or so from the road. What a relief it was to find we were all OK physically except for feeling a bit shook up!

"Well, that's that," Peter finally said. "Burst tyre and no spare wheel."

He confessed that when he collected the pick-up he could not find any spares and so he had hoped that we would not be needing any and had kept his fingers crossed to no avail. We decided that the vehicle would have to stay where it was overnight and that we would try to thumb a lift. It was still raining heavily and we looked like drowned rats. We just prayed that someone would come along as it did seem a little doubtful on such a night. However, it was not too long before we saw the headlights of a car which pulled up for us. A familiar voice shouted,

"Hello there. What's the trouble? Filthy night to break down."

It was Mr. Small, the Chairman of East African Power & Lighting Company. An embarrassed Peter replied,

"Yes, sir. Its Ellis here with my family. I wonder if you could give one or two of us a lift into town so we can get help."

We had all huddled instinctively in a position that blocked the view of one of the company's vehicles in a ditch. I don't think to this day that he ever saw the truck as he did not emerge from his car. He was very kind and said he would take me and the children. Off we went to leave Peter and Dermott sheltering in the truck.

The children and I were saturated and I felt that around me there was a decided odour of horse manure, but Mr. Small did not appear to notice. He chatted to us pleasantly, commiserating with us for breaking down on such a night. He had been playing golf at Nakuru and was on his way back to a dinner appointment in Nairobi so I asked him if he could just drop us off at a small hotel on the outskirts of town where I would be able to telephone friends who would pick us up. As he pulled up at the hotel he offered to take us home to Mitini, but I assured him we would be alright and so he left us in the foyer. I had wanted to escape for the girls and I had been trying to hold back our giggles regarding my distinctive aroma. We now giggled and laughed all the way to the telephone. We also wondered what he would have thought of the company vehicle carrying a load of horse manure.

Unbelievably, every friend I rang that night was out. We had to re-think what we could do and decided to walk a little way up the road to a garage, hoping that someone would be there. So, out into the rain we went again. Suddenly a car drew up beside us and a friendly voice shouted,

"Can I help by giving you a lift?"

It was a young man wearing a safari hat with a leopard skin band. He flung open the doors and we jumped in, so happy to escape from the rain. Then I looked around and thought, "Oh my! What have I done?". The car was decorated with zebra skin on the seats, dashboard and even on the rear window ledge. Our driver was garbed in a very flamboyant safari suit and was obviously on a bit of an alcoholic high. I stuttered and stammered about our predicament and how we were trying to get someone to take us home and pick up two men on the Nakuru road.

"Oh well, that's easy. We will all go and pick them up, there is plenty of room in this car."

I protested and said it would be fine if he just took us home but he would not listen. He said he had been looking for something to do on a wet night in Nairobi.

"You just direct me."

I was defeated and just hoped we could stay in one piece as he went tearing along at great speed.

"Whoops!" he went on, "my brakes are not very good!" as the car went into a slight skid.

"Oh no!" I shuddered. Miraculously, nothing terrible happened to us. His gaiety was infectious and I decided after all that he was really a very nice, helpful and very handsome young man.

We soon arrived at the disaster spot where I introduced him to Peter and Dermott who both seemed somewhat astonished at the sight of our new friend and rescuer and his unusual vehicle. Nevertheless, they were very glad and grateful to get away from the cheerless time they had been spending. Our new friend took us straight home where we soon recovered in the warmth and comfort. He stayed for dinner and then for the night as he told us he was on holiday. He lived in Tanganyika where his father had a tea estate and he did a little safari work, hence his rather startling outfit. He entertained us with stories of his interesting life and we were really sorry to see him go next morning. Regretfully, we never met again, but we did not forget his generous assistance on that dreadful night.

The truck was duly rescued next morning and the manure laid in the sheds. Although I did everything the text books advised, we never seemed to succeed with the mushroom venture. It was difficult to control the night temperatures and eventually I forgot the whole idea. Six months later a shamba boy dashed to the house calling excitedly for me to come and see the mushroom! I ran back with him, but to his consternation I had to tell him it was only a toadstool! And so be it. Our great efforts never produced a single mushroom.

I often think of Svend and the mushrooms. When Svend and his family finally left Kenya in the seventies he did not live long and died of cancer. His wife now lives in Nice where we once paid a visit. She is very lonely and, of course, misses his great humour and vivacity, as we all do.

Time went on. The Government had gradually restored order by their screening programme of Mau Mau followers and other Kikuyus, interning large numbers in camps. The ones they considered "safe" were undergoing a rehabilitation programme to restore them to normal life in the work force and on their shambas. In many areas womenfolk were attending courses in hygiene, child care, sewing and cooking. The courses were run by the East African Women's League, "the wild women" as they were affectionately termed by their husbands. Many of the Kikuyu girls were primitive, uneducated and not easy to instruct as they did not understand the cause and effect relationship of dirt and disease.

I was roped into the Kabete district effort when each week about thirty to forty women would turn up at each member's house in turn. We would have them out on the lawn where we duly tried to teach them how to bathe young babies correctly and keep them free from irritating flies. We taught them how to cook nourishing scones, soup and other dishes from ingredients they grew or could afford to buy. An Indian fundi made us some makeshift ovens from petrol cans which he had cleverly given a door and a shelf. We bought several of these for the girls to take home. These they stood on stones over charcoal fires with very good results. We also taught them how to make patchwork quilts from odd pieces of material to keep their children warm on cold nights and during the rainy seasons. As they progressed they were able to make dresses and skirts for themselves. Of course, we had instructors who could speak fluent Kikuyu or we would not have succeeded.

I remember, at the end of six months, we decided to give them a party at which they had to wear the clothes they had made. We baked large quantities of cakes and other goodies, arranged for them to have some entertainment and on the day we sat them round large tables and acted as waiters. Carrying a huge platter of scones, I found the first girl I came to snatching six. I laughed as I took back five and said, "One at a time please!", and thought we have not succeeded in the social graces area.

Of course it was difficult to go on permanently giving time, goods and money, so eventually we had to ask them for five shillings a year to help buy materials. Sadly, this was not a popular request and the attendance numbers dwindled very rapidly.

Around this time a dramatic discovery was made by the children when they accidentally noticed an opening in the bamboo cluster in our driveway. Being children they peered in and saw a tunnel, obviously leading into the centre. One of them went for a torch and in they went to find a clearing the size of a small room. The floor was strewn with small branches and leaves, some of them piled up into makeshift beds. In the centre was a fireplace, the usual ring of stones with old burnt out charcoal and sticks in the middle. Empty tins, corn cobs, cigarette ends and other refuse were strewn around. At first they thought to keep quiet about it and use it as a secret playhouse, but it must have had a sinister atmosphere for they came to tell us. We were plagued with the creeps as we knew it was, or had been, a Mau Mau hideout. Paddy Murphy came to inspect it and decided that it had not been used for some time; nevertheless, it was a disturbing find, and he was very thoughtful. The garden boys were ordered to chop down a very large outer area of the bamboo clump and open up the tunnel so that it would not invite any future would-be tenants. There were no more problems with it, but sometimes at night I would think about it and imagine them in there, sleeping and eating, whilst we were blissfully unaware of the danger. Still, I consoled myself, they would not have been inclined to make trouble on their own doorstep!

As the rehabilitation programme of the Kikuyu advanced, many of them were producing fruit and vegetables which began to flood the market in Nairobi. They were selling at very low prices so that when I went along with my load, the Indians were not interested unless I sold at the same figure. This, with all my overheads, I could not afford to do, and it was not long before I realised my market garden was running at a heavy loss. I racked my brain for ways to increase income as I knew that unless I did, I would have to part with quite a few of the garden staff. Suddenly I realised that if I were allowed to do so, I could sell direct to friends and housewives in the suburbs at retail prices, thus saving the day.

There was no such service of direct delivery in Nairobi. On enquiring at the City Hall if I needed a licence I caused quite a few raised eyebrows and some considerable consternation. It was unheard of, there was no precedent - who is this crazy woman? How can she contemplate such a thing? In the circumstances, however, they agreed there was no law to stop me going ahead. This crazy woman loved the life at Mitini and also did not wish to see loyal, hard-working staff thrown out of work, so it was with great zest we all helped to organise the new venture.

Andrea and I would set off in the early mornings with a loaded van, some scales and a money box, which Andrea would clasp on his knees as if guarding the crown jewels. We did marvellously well apart from a few frights from watchdogs in the early days when Andrea would come galloping back down a driveway with one attached to his heel! These rather scary episodes were soon overcome by customers, anxious to partake of our services, locking up their dogs when they knew we were due. We returned home at lunch time each day with an empty van and a box full of lovely cash which was more than ample to keep things going. We were happy, our customers were delighted with the really fresh garden produce and I was able to congratulate myself on the wonderful success of the scheme.

The happy days, however, were not to last. The blow fell when one day I received a letter from the Town Clerk informing me that I must cease forthwith from selling vegetables at retail price from a motor vehicle. There was to be a meeting of the Chamber of Commerce at which it would be decided if I would be allowed a licence or not. Sad to say, when the answer came, it was in the negative. I think the suburban shopkeepers found that I was taking away all their customers and that, of course, I must be stopped.

Now I was really frustrated and defeated; regretfully we came to the end of market gardening, and were forced to part with quite a few staff, which was very upsetting. The old adage that when the Lord shuts a door he opens a window came true in the respect that our two year lease on Mitini was almost up. Wondering if we should re-lease, the answer came when Mr. Mitchell called to say that he wanted to sell Mitini. He gave us first option to buy and really pressed us to take the place as he knew we loved it. Tempting as the offer was, we knew that we might not stay in Nairobi permanently as Peter's company could transfer him at the end of each three years to any of the East African territories, and as they also provided housing or rent in lieu, there was no real need for us to own a property in Kenya. It was a heartbreaking decision to move on and leave all our garden staff and friends in the district. The property was eventually sold to an estate agent who changed it into a housing estate of two and a half acre blocks on which purchasers erected very nice homes; but I'm glad we were the last people to enjoy it as a complete estate with its attendant gracious lifestyle.

Even today as I have nostalgic thoughts of Kenya, I always think of Mitini as the place where we were the happiest.

CHAPTER THIRTEEN

BACK TO CITY LIFE

With sadness in our hearts, we packed to leave Mitini. Dermott's widowed mother came out from England and he set up a home for her near the Ngong Hills. He had been a great friend and was to remain so for many years. Our livestock was a problem, but we managed to find someone to look after the horses; the rest we had unhappily to part with. For the next eighteen months or so we were to live in a maisonette and then another attractive house in the city of Nairobi.

These were the years when Peter was very busy designing and supervising electrical installations for many new buildings and factories going up in Nairobi, Kampala, Nakuru, Dar-es-Salaam, Moshi and even Zanzibar. The girls and I were lucky to occasionally travel with him, a recompense for losing the open air life of Mitini, and so we became familiar with most of the three territories of East Africa and made a large circle of friends who were always pleased to have us for holidays and week-ends at their homes.

Other week-ends were often spent on picnic trips with local friends to places such as the Ngong Hills and other scenically beautiful areas. One of these was to the Rift Valley, where we received another unexpected Mau Mau fright. We had just unloaded all the food, set out the table and chairs, lit the primus stove on which the kettle was merrily boiling, when we heard gun shots not far away. A car came into sight being driven at a crazy speed. The driver slowed down as he swerved past us shouting,

"Get out of here. There's a gang of Mau Mau up there, all armed. They'll be down here any minute."

I have never seen a group of people move as fast as we did, throwing everything back in the cars and shooting away. The primus stove and kettle were left as a souvenir for the Mau Mau, a small price to pay for getting away safely. This sort of event always depressed us when to all intents and purposes Kenya was supposedly now under 'control'.

The time gradually came along for our first home leave to England which naturally was a great event to look forward to, filling us with excitement and anticipation. This time we flew on a larger plane which called at Wadi Halfa on the border of Sudan and Egypt for a night stop. We landed on a desert strip where, waiting to take us to an hotel on the banks of the Nile, were several Arab taxi drivers. One would not have expected to be scared of a drive in the wide open desert but, as the taxi drivers took off, they decided to have a race. As we careered along, hitting concealed rocks in the sand and almost turning over several times, we were almost frightened out of our wits. The drivers thought it all a great joke and as we laughed with them at the end of the journey, I suspect they realised it was with great relief. It was so much more pleasurable having Peter along with us on this trip. We have memories of the little white hotel surrounded by shrubs, mostly poinsettia, and the houseboat anchored in the Nile at the bottom of the garden which took any overflow of guests. We were given rooms in the hotel on this occasion and we spent a very enjoyable evening with our fellow travellers.

Next morning at dawn after a cup of tea in bed, we were rushed back to the little airstrip for an early take-off. The taxi drivers were more subdued in the chill morning air. As the sun came up over the hills we drove past the mud walled houses of the little town and caught glimpses of residents preparing to enter a new day. I'm glad we saw Wadi Halfa before the building of the Aswan Dam for it was a pleasant, peaceful oasis.

In the three years we had spent in Kenya, the flight from Nairobi to London had been cut from three days to two, owing to improvements in aircraft performance. We were sorry about this in a way, as it meant on our second day we only landed at Benghazi to refuel and then flew straight on to London. It was late in the evening as we emerged from London airport after checking out at Customs. As the officer passed our duty free brandy, he joked,

"You'll be needing that!"

We went on to an hotel in the city where we shivered all night. I remember the month was May, and what an exceptionally cold May it was. I don't think we were ever warm during the whole of our stay in England because all our relatives had "spring cleaned", after which, of course, they never light fires. Central heating and electric blankets were still comforts of the future.

Next day London looked dirty and terribly overcrowded, and although we knew all the pleasures and treasures that lay behind that drab exterior, we took off for the provinces. What reunions we had with all our relatives and friends who, at first, were a little hesitant and withdrawn, as if they expected us to have changed or grown away from them during our absence in a new land. One of them exclaimed,

"But you are still the same, you haven't changed a bit!"

"Of course we are," I surprisedly answered. "Why would we be different? It's us."

England seemed so tiny after the wide open spaces of Africa, with its little hedgerowed fields and pocket handkerchief gardens. We felt hemmed in; the crowds of people and all the traffic in the cities overpowered and dismayed us, despite the fact that we had lived with them for years and never noticed before we went to Kenya. Africa was already under our skin!

The weeks slipped away as we explored Britain and visited everyone. Our great sadness was leaving the grandparents when it was time to return.

"Why don't you come out on holiday to see us," we begged, "you would love Kenya."

But they never came, in all the years we lived there.

"England is good enough for us," they would say, as if a visit overseas was a traitorous act. I think the truth really was that they were scared of flying and felt too old to cope with all the necessary arrangements.

We returned to Kenya via Benghazi and Khartoum, all very uneventfully and as we circled Nairobi airport prior to landing I thought how good it was to be coming 'home'. By the expressions on the faces of my husband and children I knew they too had the same thought.

A very sad event took place just after our return. The Johnstones, our good friends and neighbours at Mitini, suffered a terrible bereavement with the death of Johnnie. Dear Johnnie, who had fallen in the cactus the night of the Mau Mau raid and with whom we had spent so many happy hours. Peter walked in home one morning about 10am looking extremely ashen and shaken, almost in tears.

"Whatever is it?" I exclaimed, "are you ill? Has there been an accident?"

"No, no, I'm sorry to give you a fright dear," he replied, "but it's Johnnie. He died in hospital during the night."

"Oh no! He can't have," I gasped. "I spoke to him only yesterday."

"Well, he had a cerebral haemorrhage about seven o'clock last night and never came round. They got him into hospital and I believe he died about midnight. Diana's parents have just let me know; they have asked if we can go round to give a hand with the funeral arrangements as it will be held at 4pm today."

"Oh my dear!" I collapsed. "I can't believe it. Poor Diana, poor children. What a terrible thing."

"Yes I know dear," Peter comforted, "but come on now. We must get over there to see what we can do."

As we drove over I thought of Johnnie, a charming, loveable, extremely gifted man, ex-Army Intelligence officer, who had later joined Special Branch Police in Kenya where he had been involved in rounding up the Mau Mau. He had written one book on his experiences as a prisoner of war in World War II, which was a success, and had been busy writing a second one. How could he be gone!

What a sorrowful day that was. Death in Kenya always seemed so relentless, where the funeral is held within twenty-four hours, but maybe it was a blessing in disguise to have so much to do and see to in those early hours of bereavement. Johnnie's three children aged ten, nine and only eighteen months, were fully aware of the situation for they had seen their father fall in the sitting room, and later the ambulance taking him away for ever. They were inconsolable; at least the two eldest, although Richard the baby sensed something dreadfully amiss with his usual placid existence. I spent the day keeping him amused, and listening to the other two talking of their past happy days with their dear daddy. We all went along to the funeral where they were very brave and dignified for it was a military funeral. Military funerals are always very moving but this time, as the Last Post was sounded, my heart ached for all Johnnie's lost years; he was only 38 at the time of his death.

And so we lost and missed a very dear friend. Diana took her children to Njoro to recover a little, after which she struggled to work and care for them. She married again some time later and made a new life.

After this unsettling occurrence, Peter decided to take us away for a break. We knew one of the first white hunters in Kenya, Bob Foster, who had a farm on the slopes of Kilimanjaro. Luckily he had sent us a kind invitation to visit as he was at home between safaris. It was a truly interesting interval, and we never tired of listening to his stories of adventures, with many notable clients, as we sat around a huge log fire in the evenings. One of the saddest things he told us was how each year the Government had to hire hunters to cull the elephants in the Voi area, as they were destroying all the crops. He too was upset as he related how many he shot each week.

Many famous and interesting people lived and farmed in West Kilimanjaro, including the Stirlings of World War II fame. Hardy Kruger, the film star, built an attractive tourist lodge there in idyllic surroundings at which we stayed once in later years. At the time, it was still rather damp weather after the rainy season, and I remember we made a trip through the lower forest area of Mt. Meru, the sister mountain to Mt. Kilimanjaro, on a rather hazardous track which led us up past turbulent streams and waterfalls to the Ngurdoto National Park. The main feature of this park is an extinct crater which had returned to natural vegetation in which lived many species of wild animals. One could stand on the rim of the crater engrossed in this panoramic spectacle without disturbing the inhabitants, an unusual and satisfying way of game viewing. However, to reach the crater, we had to ascend a difficult and steep track of treacherous, slippery mud, in which at one stage, we slipped back several yards. Then followed a grating thump on the roof of the car and the shock of seeing the same roof bending dangerously near our heads. Peter dared not stop and on arrival at the summit we found that something had hit us with devastating results. As we descended at the end of our visit, we found this to be the stump of a tree protruding sideways from the bank at the side of the road, obviously too low for the comfort of passing vehicles! The car looked a sorry wreck as we drove into the grounds of the lodge where fellow visitors thought we must have had an accident in which the car had overturned. An expensive item to repair but the outing was well worth the inconvenience.

Gradually, as the days went by, I could feel 'change' in the air. Peter was restless. I was not surprised when he told me that the head of the large engineering company he had worked for in England was coming out to Kenya to assess the possibility of setting up a company. We were to entertain and help him. At the end of his visit he offered Peter the Managing Directorship of the new company he had decided to establish in Nairobi. He was of the opinion that Kenya was now politically "safe" with the Mau Mau element under control and predicted a boom period of investment and growth in the colony.

Of course, Peter was very excited with the offer and the challenge, and he applied himself to the task of dealing with the necessary arrangements. This change-over meant that our residential status in Kenya would no longer be on contract terms but that we would now be residents of Kenya. As we would be living in the Nairobi area I thought wistfully of Mitini but it was too late and one cannot change past decisions.

Work for the new company poured in; the staff - European, Asian and African was regularly increased to deal with this influx. It was a hectic time for Peter who spent long hours at his office and entertaining clients. We had many Sikh electricians who vied with each other in their efforts to please. They carried gifts to our doors which we had to discourage. They invited us to their homes for curry lunches which we accepted, but we almost burst with food and drink in our attempts not to disappoint them. However, we did develop a great liking for prawn curry.

A complication of these busy days was a period of ill health for Valerie, our second daughter, who grew thinner every day. Visits to doctors and specialists ended in negative tests for all kinds of diseases. A specialist then decided to remove her appendix but she did not improve in health. Eventually further tests revealed that she had amoebic dysentery. She spent a very unhappy time in hospital having treatment after which she gradually recovered. She and Elaine were now attending the Loreto Convent school where they stayed for the remainder of their school days, a place they really loved. The nuns were so devoted to their task of educationally training the young girls, and most of all assisting to mould their characters, which resulted in the helpful, courteous human beings they are today. Some of the old nuns still write letters to us.

We took a brief holiday at the coast to help along Val's convalescence, renting a house so that we could take our pets along. We had acquired an African hare which was Val's proud possession. He was so tame, sleeping with the cats or on Val's bed if she could smuggle him in. He loved to join us on our evening walks along the beach, after which he would snuggle up to our feet or jump up on the settee for a cuddle. We had him for a long time and then unfortunately he succumbed to pneumonia from a chill he received in the rainy season and we missed him terribly.

Although Kenya was now a much safer place to live, there were still odd raids at lonely farms and estates by the Mau Mau terrorists who had not surrendered. Our last memory of one of these was when we visited some friends at a sisal estate at Makuyu. We were about to have lunch when the peaceful, sunny day was shattered by loud shouting and gun fire coming from the direction of the labour lines. Reg, our friend, went off with Peter to investigate, leaving his wife, myself and our children locked in the house.

"Here we go again," I thought, "when will it all end?"

One was always so scared when the menfolk ventured out into unknown danger. However, luckily, it was soon all over. The men returned to say the loyal staff of the estate had managed to chase them off and there were no casualties.

The new company prospered in its early years and Peter was kept extremely busy. We began to feel part of the settler community of Kenya, as opposed to the "two or three year wonders" the settlers termed people on contract. But perhaps even then there was a vague rustle of the winds of change which were later to hit Africa. The settlers did not feel all that secure and called for some assurance that their future would be safeguarded. They marched on Government House demanding some word from Whitehall on the situation.

Representatives of the British Government were sent out to speak at a meeting in Nairobi City Hall. Peter and I went along to listen to words of encouragement and reassurance that we could all go back to our homes, businesses and farms and rest in peace; carry on working and investing for Britain would never relinquish her strategically important colony of Kenya!

On the strength of this statement we began to think of finding or building ourselves a permanent home in Kenya.

CHAPTER FOURTEEN

WE MEET ARMAND AND MICHAELA DENIS

Weekends became fully occupied searching for a place of our own. We had a great desire to find this somewhere facing the Ngong Hills, as they had captured our imagination from the very first moment we saw them, especially as one of the first books we read on arrival in Kenya was Baroness von Blixen's "Out of Africa".

I knew exactly what she felt when she wrote her opening sentence...

"I had a farm in Africa at the foot of the Ngong Hills..." and later carries on..." a landscape that had not its like in all the world. It was Africa distilled up through six thousand feet, like the strong and refined essence of a continent. The colours were dry and burnt like the colours in pottery, the views were immensely wide. Everything that you saw made for greatness and freedom, and unequalled nobility."

How wonderfully she described it.

For several months we searched in vain except for finding one grown up plot on the last hillside facing the Masai plains, from which one looked straight across at the Ngongs, but we could not discover who owned it. Providence, however, seems to resolve many things in life, as one day we were chatting casually with residents in that district when one of them happened to say,

"I wonder if Armand Denis would part with his plot. He has had it for years, I think with the intention of using it as a small animal reserve, but he has never done anything with it. Why don't you call and see him? He lives not far from the plot, just down the road there."

We were delighted to find that this was the plot we had been enquiring about for so long and were grateful to receive the information. Still, we hesitated. Would a world famous, wildlife personality such as Armand Denis have bought the land except for some specific purpose? We sat in the car, dithering with the idea of calling on him, when Peter said,

"Oh well, why not? He can say 'yes' or 'no', but if we don't ask him we'll never know."

And so we were to enter a new chapter in our lives as we knocked on the door of the Denis' home. It was partly ajar; we heard a female voice from an inner distance calling,

"Come in, come in."

We stepped into a large hall which had several doors and in the centre a beautiful timbered staircase with wrought iron balustrades. This we saw led up to a large landing with wide French windows which were open. We hesitated and then heard the call,

"Come upstairs, I'm up here on the balcony."

This was how we met Michaela Denis. She was resting on a couch and excused herself for not greeting us downstairs as she had just come out of hospital. We apologised for disturbing her but she assured us we were very welcome, asking us to sit down and chat as she was very pleased to have company; Armand Denis was away and the staff were taking their afternoon rest period.

We admired the house and the view from her balcony which was across a wooded valley, the trees framing the Ngongs in the background. She said they had their living quarters upstairs to get the full benefit of this beautiful view. Michaela obviously had a genuine interest in people as she asked all about us and how we liked living in Kenya, which she adored. It became quite easy for Peter to explain the reason for our visit, after which she sat looking at us thoughtfully for some time. Then her expression suddenly confirmed that she had made a snap decision.

"Look," she said, "Armand is away, but I would like you to come to dinner on Sunday to meet him. I will have persuaded him by then to sell you the block providing you will promise me one thing."

"And I wonder what that would be?" enquired Peter.

She smiled.

"Well, OK! We are going off filming in the Far East shortly for a year or so, and if you will promise me that you will live in this house and caretake things for us for that period, then I can promise you the plot. Look how well it would work out too. You could build your house while we are away, and you would be close by to supervise, so everything would work out beautifully for you and us."

We were fascinated by the quickness of her mind, and somewhat taken aback. We seemed destined to be offered other peoples' luxurious homes. My first reaction was a slight fear of the responsibility of caring for this large property, but the offer was tempting in so far as we knew she had accepted us as potential purchasers. We wanted the plot so badly that I agreed we would come along the following Sunday. We met Armand Denis who was a charming man. He put no obstacles in our path and the sale went through smoothly.

So once again we were thrown into the turmoil of moving house. This time, however, we had the excitement of knowing our very own home would emerge just where we had always wanted it to be. Thanks to Michaela.

The Denis establishment kept us occupied and intrigued. It was a spacious house of Portuguese design; the walls were of stone, painted white, both inside and outside. It was furnished with valuable antiques and interesting carvings and curios picked up on their various travels. Michaela had a delightfully feminine study with pretty cushions, Dresden china and crystal lamps. This was situated over the well of the staircase and hall. One side of it was just a low wall topped by a carved wrought iron screen, through which one could see everyone coming up or down the stairs. I spent many relaxing, quiet hours in that little room. At each side of the staircase there were again only low walls with stone arches which were filled with the same decorative wrought iron panels. The lounge was huge, with many tall windows and a stone fireplace, over which hung a picture of Michaela nursing a leopard. In fact this picture was the book cover of 'Leopard in My Lap', one of the books she had written. The dining room on the other side was equally pleasing, backed by kitchens and stores. Below on the ground floor were bedrooms, bathrooms and the workrooms where Armand edited his own films.

They had left behind fourteen cats and three dogs, several birds in large aviaries, the odd animal or two in cages and best loved of all, Minnie the Mongoose. Minnie had featured in lots of childrens' programmes on TV in America and England. She was a great delight to us all, and had the run of the house during the day. At night she slept in her own special house outside. She loved to creep out from under beds and chairs, giving one's ankle a quick nip when she wished to attract attention.

Next door lived Des Bartlett, the Denis' chief cameraman, with his wife Jen and daughter Julie. Des has become very famous in his own right over the years with such films and books as 'Flight of the Snow Geese' and 'Nature's Paradise'. He was a perfectionist cameraman.

In the grounds of their home was a large wired enclosure where many animals, birds and even snakes were kept for short periods as they were needed for close up shots for the 'On Safari' series of films which were then being produced. Feeding them all and keeping everything clean involved a great deal of work. It was a fascinating place. We were called round many times to be introduced to newcomers in the enclosure. The Bartlett family had no fear at all of the occupants and walked in and out completely at ease, but it was a new experience for us to have baboons jumping on our heads and pelicans creeping up behind us to peck at our legs! Our favourites were two chimpanzees, Charlie and Bridget, who often came over to our house where they entertained us with their antics. Charlie liked to join in at meal times, drinking from a mug and sampling all the fare which caused much amusement. Bridget had a wardrobe of clothes for filming. She liked nothing better than dressing and undressing like some experienced model. There were baby lions, baby cheetahs, a Grant's gazelle, an aardvark, lots of buck and many other animals. We were privileged to become part of this very interesting organisation, adding greatly to our knowledge of the habits of the wildlife of Kenya.

The domestic cats and dogs had cages of their own in which they slept at night. We had a near tragedy one night with the cats, and our first experience of an attack by African safari ants. After visiting the theatre and returning home, we heard loud screams and meowing from the cats' cage. On rushing to the scene we found to our great horror that several chains of ants, thicker than a man's arm, as they clustered in their thousands, had entered the cage. The poor cats were swinging from the wire at the top of the cage like small monkeys; they were terrified and in great pain from large numbers of ants attacking and trying to devour them. We ran for insect sprays but these were pathetically ineffective. Sending for help next door, we were relieved to find Nick Pickford, one of the staff, rushing to our aid. He was armed with a blow lamp, explaining that this was the only way to deal with such a concerted attack, as he commenced to incinerate them. It took him hours to destroy them as the chains led right down into the valley and up the other side to the plains. We rescued the cats from the cage, suffering in the process from many bites ourselves. The poor creatures were hysterical from their torture; ants were embedded in their fur, eyes, noses and rear ends. It was an impossible task to try and pick them off, and I suddenly thought of water, a bath of water. We ran to the bathroom, gently put the cats in tepid water and miraculously most of the ants floated away from their victims. Thankfully we were able to save all of them by rubbing them dry with towels, dressing their wounds and giving them drinks of warm milk. They seemed no worse off next day for their dreadful experience.

We had previously heard stories of safari ant attacks and how some people had armies of them going through their houses at night, for once they set off in a certain direction, nothing will deter them. If a house is in the way, then through it they will go. An old settler gave me a tip of sprinkling ordinary white flour across the doorsteps in the rainy season when they are more prevalent. This clogged up their feelers and so further movement was impossible.

These ants, too, had been known to attack small babies in their prams if left unattended, possibly attracted by the dried sweet milk round their mouths. Not very pleasant little creatures as their bite is savage. We also experienced their fierce bites when gardening at times and would shed clothes and shoes, regardless of spectators, to get rid of them as hastily as possible.

The Denis' houseboy stayed on with us and worked in very well with our staff. He was a friendly, jolly Jaluo who gave us no trouble. On his day off he would cycle into Nairobi to meet his friends.

Charles came to a very sad end. When cycling home one night he became the victim of a hit and run driver. He was found dead in a ditch with his bicycle on top of him, after we made enquiries as to why he did not turn up on duty next morning. We were all so upset and shocked. Sacunda sadly shaking his head kept repeating,

"Shauri ya Mungu Memsahib, shauri ya Mungu." (It's God's will, memsahib, God's will.)

We were to have a second blow with the death of our beloved Alsatian, Lassie, when she was giving birth to puppies. Septicaemia was diagnosed, but not in time, and so sadly we had to bury her in the valley below the house. There were many tears and recriminations; she was such a wonderful dog with a loving nature, and this event left a sad and hollow gap in our lives.

A lighter note was the affair of the missing eggs. We had reinstalled hens who lived in one of the large vacant animal cages. Months went by with no sign of an egg. Someone suggested they were perhaps being stolen, so we padlocked the gate. Still no eggs! However, some time later we found a broken egg on the floor of the cage which was a mystery as, if the thief had been an animal such as a mongoose, then the yolk would have been missing. One day we set off for town, but discovering something forgotten we returned to the house. The mystery was now solved, for we discovered the thief so intent on the job that he never heard the car slowly pulling up behind him. We were spellbound, watching one of our casual garden staff holding a long bamboo pole, at the end of which a large spoon was firmly attached. This he had ingeniously inserted through the wire and into the laying boxes. By devious twists and turns he was extracting the eggs one by one and popping them into his upturned hat! His dexterity and patience were something to behold. Gradually the funny side of things hit us and we roared with laughter, giving away the fact that we were interested spectators. What a fright he received; he was too shaken to move and so Peter was able to give him an almighty lecture and dispense with his temporary services at the same time. Once again we had fresh eggs for breakfast, and whilst eating them, often thought of our clever friend and surmised that perhaps he had a hangover the morning he had dropped one!

During this period we met many well-known personalities. People from the BBC such as David Attenborough, who were involved with the Denis' in wildlife film making. We also met Dr. Louis Leakey and his family who lived just round the corner. The boys were very young then, but one of them already had a small snake park in the garden which I gave a very wide berth. Joy Adamson was another visitor who impressed us with her absolute immunity to any kind of fear when dealing with wild animals. She was a real character.

Despite our intense interest and involvement in this exciting world of wildlife, we nevertheless managed to get on with the clearing of our plot. An architect friend had drawn up the plans and specification for a large two storey house, also a small guest house in which we had decided to camp if the big one was not ready by the time the Denis' returned. The buildings would be of stone which was being delivered from a nearby quarry. The site for the main house was chosen on the rim of the hill where we had found we could see the Ngongs clearly, but where, too, there was an uninterrupted view of Kilimanjaro. Who could wish for more! We, like the Denis', now decided to have our living rooms upstairs in order to enjoy this panorama to its full extent.

Maureen's school days were gradually nearing completion. A friend, Charles Hayes, talked with Peter about a career for her in the newspaper world. The Aga Khan was interested in launching a Swahili daily newspaper in Kenya to be called 'Taifa Leo' (Daily Nation). She was very interested and subsequently became a staff member of the initial team. Because she was the youngest, she was allowed, at the opening ceremony, to press the button for the machinery to turn out the first copy of Taifa Leo. A great thrill for a young girl.

So, the days flew by and the Denis' returned from their long and tiring tour. Michaela brought us exotic little souvenirs from the Far East. She was delighted to be back in Kenya and her own home again. We had to move along to our small house as the large one was not quite completed. The quarters were a little cramped after the Denis mansion, but we hardly noticed, so intent were we on planning the lay-out for the gardens, the building of stables and outbuildings, and the decorations and furnishings for the big house, with the resultant enjoyment and satisfaction that only one's very own place can bestow.

CHAPTER FIFTEEN

HOME?

Armand Denis came to call on us in our new home. He had always shown an interest in the girls, so the purpose of his visit was to ask if we thought Maureen might be interested in learning film editing. There was a great deal of work to be done as a result of his visit to the Far East, hence he needed an assistant. However, he said that editors were born, not made, and that if Maureen did not have the flair, then after three months he would have to tell her so.

Maureen at this time was very happy in the newspaper world so the decision was left to her. However, the enticing glamour of the film industry won her over and she was soon engrossed in her new work at the Denis establishment. Within a few weeks Armand again called to say he was delighted with her ability and that he hoped she would stay with him for many years. She did stay for over five years and later had the great satisfaction of seeing her name credited on many Armand Denis Productions' films.

Our neighbours at the new house were Mr. Michael O'Rourke, the Kenya Commissioner of Police and Mr. Frank Bailey, both living alone in their respective dwellings. Always friendly and helpful, we found them very interesting personalities. Frank Bailey, an ex-Army Intelligence Officer, was writing a book on his experiences after the war as a Control Officer for the Desert Locust Organisation for Africa, which had its headquarters in Nairobi. He had been stationed in all parts of East Africa, Ethiopia, Somalia and the Hadhramaut in Arabia. His book, 'Harry the Locust', when completed, made very amusing reading.

Frank lived very simply. He had built three houses which were rented out to provide him with an income, and in the corner of the third one's five acre garden, he had erected a makeshift home for himself which he called "Chatsworth"! It was a fascinating place built, I think, from all the left-over building materials from the three houses, so was a kind of house that Jack built. The roof was part shingle, part tiled and part asbestos. The windows were of mixed variety and size, some with wooden and some with steel frames. The tiled floors of the rooms were, like Jacob's coat, of many colours. But a really attractive olde worlde front porch, complete with rambling rose, gave the residence a welcoming and homely appearance. He had been used to camping out for many years so his bathroom was outside - just a bamboo walled shelter with the usual bucket on a lever; his toilet was a long drop at the bottom of the garden.

Many evenings he would call us over to have a sundowner beer with him. He had a large easy chair; sometimes in fine weather this would be out on the front porch. This chair had a shelf attached at each side, one for the full bottles and one for the empties! He kept poultry and had a tame hen named Blondie who would perch on the arm of his chair each time he sat down, blissfully content. She was most agitated and unhappy when he got up to wander away.

He eventually succumbed to building a more civilised bathroom in the cold, wet season which we were called upon to inspect and christen. He had knocked out part of one of his bedroom walls and built three outer walls in a rectangle, where proudly displayed stood a large bath and a toilet, each professionally attached to the appropriate piping. After imbibing that evening I was asked to have the first honour of paying a call. Dutifully I went off, only finding on sitting down that the new extension had not been given a roof so I received a free shower too from the heavy rain. That was Frank!

My time was fully occupied supervising the layout of our gardens. We had taken on extra staff and a head gardener named John who took great interest in all the plans, so we soon had beautiful rockeries surrounding the guest house and bougainvillaea creeping up the verandah pillars. Many large indigenous trees gave the grounds a finished look, but there was still a great deal to do. The Africans working on the big house were living in our quarters; they worked long hours from dawn to dusk to hurry along the completion of the job, and the hillsides resounded with their hammering, shouting, singing and laughter.

One day Frank Bailey came over to let us know that lions had visited his garden the previous evening, chewing up his garden hoses and also the tyres on his car, so warned us to keep a lookout for them.

The Old Sub Chief.

Sketch by Louise Ellis

The Author.

Cheetah

Peter with Valerie and Elaine in later years.

On the occasion of the inauguration of the Republic of Kenya

Their Excellencies The President
and Mrs Kenyatta

request the pleasure of the company of

Mr & Mrs Ellis

at a Garden Party

at State House, on Monday, 14th December 1964, at 4.00 p.m.

R.S.V.P.
The Social Secretary

Please bring this card with you

State House
Box 530, Nairobi

An invitation to the Inauguration Garden Party.

A Masai warrior.

Masai herd boys on the Ngong Hills.

Valerie and Elaine make friends on Safari with a Masai mother
and children.

A farewell to Local Government.

Val's farewell walk at Anmer House prior to leaving for Australia.

Zebra in Game Park.

Lions in Nairobi Game Park.

Maureen with 'Charlie the Chimp'.

Elaine, Valerie and Maureen with a new playmate.

Our horses had been acting up in the evenings, seemingly on edge and nervous so, now we knew the reason, we made sure they were safely locked in their stables each night. Sure enough we soon received a visit which gave John the fright of his life. He lived in a wooden hut which had a glass window and a not very secure front door. On returning there in the evening he suddenly heard growls and gruntings not very far away. Peeping through his window, after slamming shut the front door, he saw four lions busily exploring our grounds. He watched helplessly as they chewed up all the garden hoses. Now they advanced on his home; they sniffed at the hut, following this action by rubbing themselves vigorously on the walls, causing the building to shake and tremble. John fervently hoped that it would stand up to this heavy treatment and that they would not attack the door. He dare not move except to glance out of the window when he heard no further movement. They must have eaten well that day for now he found that they had all gone to sleep, one of them lying right across the entrance. John sat on a chair all night, not daring to make a sound or try to escape. At daybreak they stirred, shook themselves and prepared to depart. The greatest indignity as far as John was concerned, on top of no sleep, was the fact that all of them urinated on the corner of his hut as they left to wander away down the valley! After the great strain of the night John was gratified to find us anxious and ready listeners to his tale of hours of terror, and only gradually relaxed during the day as he repeated it to all and sundry.

We decided something must be done when we heard of other neighbours receiving calls, so we got in touch with the Chief Game Warden at Nairobi National Park who was able to arrange a round up of stray lions. Eventually they were inveigled into the park, and we were all able to relax.

Maureen was very happy by this time in her new career. She loved the animals, being particularly fond of some new baby cheetahs who followed the Denis family and staff around like pet dogs. Also, she had become friendly with many of the young people interested in wild life filming, some of whom came to work for Armand Denis for short periods: Alan Root, Hugo van Lawick, who later married Jane Goodall, the girl famous for living with and filming chimpanzees, Nick Pickford and Simon Trevor. The Leakey boys were always near. Des and Jen Bartlett taught her a great deal about photography and she spent many happy hours engrossed in helping them to sort some of

Des' magnificent stills for books which would be published over the years.

One evening Peter and I received a visitor; young Richard Leakey who at the time was fourteen years of age. He arrived in a landrover and was smoking a pipe! He had come to ask if he could escort Maureen to a cinema in Nairobi as there was a good film being shown there. Peter and I exchanged amused glances.

"Would you like a beer with that smoke?" asked Peter in mischievous mood. Richard said he would love one. Maureen had not yet arrived home from work, but when she did we all managed to persuade him to go back home as he would surely be picked up by the police. Of course, he had been driving for some years in the quiet country lanes round his home and also down at Olduvai Gorge where his parents worked as he went down there to help them during school holidays.

Not long after this visit, he and Maureen had a rather scary adventure with the cheetahs. As they were now getting quite large and had become more unmanageable they had been placed in an enclosure in a fenced meadow behind the Bartlett's house. There was a shelter for them in the enclosure and various items which kept them amused. The African staff fed them meat each evening. Roaming in the meadow was a young pet Grant's gazelle. The Denis' and the Bartletts had to go off to help and to film 'Operation Noah' in Rhodesia at the time when the dam there overflowed and many wild animals were being drowned. They wanted to join the rescue team. Maureen drove them to the airport and after waving them good-bye she returned to her work. Very shortly after this, an African came tearing up to tell her that the cheetahs were not in their enclosure. He could not see them anywhere or the Grant's gazelle. She went with him to the meadow and over to the enclosure where she found the gate open. She asked him if he had left it open and he said no, and that he thought that the last person who fed them must have been careless and left the gate unfastened. Feeling responsible, Maureen continued walking through the long grass in the meadow. The African drew back saying,

"No Memsahib, don't go in there."

She kept on walking and to her horror found the Grant's gazelle lying dead in the grass. Then she turned and saw the cheetahs not far away resting in the shade under a tree. They hissed and spat, got up in a menacing manner and started advancing towards her. She very quickly realised that they must have succumbed to their natural hunting instincts and had killed the gazelle. They must not have been hungry at the time and so had left it to rest in the shade until evening. However, they were guarding it and she knew that they would injure or even kill anyone who tried to move it. She backed away from the gazelle, talking to the cheetahs as she did so, and gradually was able to dash out of the meadow.

With everyone away except the African staff, she decided to ring the Chief Warden of Nairobi National Game Park. Unluckily, she was told that he was not in his office, so she rang the Leakey house. Only Richard was at home. He said he would come at once to see if he could help. He was a very self assured, confident young boy and said he had a plan. He would take a panga and some ropes in a landrover and that he would back the vehicle right up to the gazelle, taking Maureen in the passenger seat. Then, if they succeeded in getting that far, he wanted Maureen to take the wheel whilst he crept out round the back where he would attempt to throw the gazelle into the landrover. He would then jump in and cut some pieces of meat from the animal, tie them to the ropes and sling them out to trail behind. They would then drive past the cheetahs and slowly into the enclosure with the cheetahs hopefully following their kill. Hopefully, by this time too, the cheetahs would be feeling hungry and would attack the meat which would give them the chance to cut the ropes free, drive out, and slam the gate.

If I had known all this was happening, I would have had a heart attack I'm sure, but Maureen did not inform us. Amazingly, Richard's plan worked. They drove to the gazelle, Maureen took the wheel and kept the engine running whilst Richard carried out the task of preparing the meat. The cheetahs were used to seeing landrovers and probably recognised Maureen, but it was the noise of Maureen revving the engine now and again that appeared to keep them mesmerised. They then drove slowly past the cheetahs but they did not move at first, so Maureen reversed, feeling some terror, and now they got up and followed. All was over very shortly after that and they escaped back to the house. The Africans then went in and strengthened the enclosure and its gate and all was well. What an experience!

Calling in at Peter's office one afternoon, I was amazed to find a large vervet monkey chained to a leg of the desk.

"Whatever is he doing here?" I exclaimed.

Peter looked at me sheepishly and said,

"Oh, old Tarsem Singh is going back to India and can't find a home for him. He's had him for years and doesn't want to have him put down, so I said I would take him."

"Oh Peter, I don't know. Would it be a good idea? I don't really like vervets and you know Armand Denis always said only have gibbons for a pet, never trust any of the others. Couldn't he go to the game park?"

He didn't look a very good tempered monkey to me and I eyed him suspiciously.

"Well, I don't know", Peter replied. "He's been tame a long time and may not survive out there in the park."

I could see he meant to keep him.

"Well, the children would enjoy him I'm sure," he followed on a little lamely.

The vervet was trundled into the back of the station wagon where he was uncomfortable and snapped and snarled in protest all the way home.

"Now where are you going to put him?" I asked, as Peter dragged him by the chain into the garden.

"Don't fuss dear. We'll fix up a long running chain for him and he'll get plenty of exercise that way and not be a nuisance."

John came to the rescue and he and Peter worked until dark making sure the vervet was comfortably accommodated. The girls were quite pleased at the novelty of keeping a monkey and took turns at feeding him with bananas and other food, and for quite some time all went well. He seemed to be happy, chattering and jabbering away all day. He would entertain us in the evenings, showing off with various antics, but we never felt happy about releasing him from the chain for he was not a very biddable monkey, and we were afraid of offending the neighbours.

One evening, Elaine went to feed him, as usual, when for no apparent reason, he smartly bit her right through the palm of the hand, quite savagely. We had to rush her off to hospital for medical attention and injections. Luckily, she had no ill effects.

"Don't you think we should get rid of him Peter?" I pleaded after this event.

"Yes, I guess we should," he agreed. "I'll ask around at work to see if any of the other chaps would like him. If not, we will have to think of something else."

We were now a little nervous of him at feeding times, although we kept up a friendly atmosphere, but Elaine kept her distance! The following Saturday afternoon he gave us a horrible shock when we discovered that he had escaped. We had not missed him, but our garden staff had heard him chattering away in the topmost branches of a very large tree in Mr. O'Rourke's garden.

"Oh gracious! What can we do?" I shouted to the others.

Mr. O'Rourke was not at home for which we were thankful, and so we hoped to rescue the monkey before his return. Our garden boys, along with Mr. O'Rourke's staff gathered at the foot of the tree. They called for him to come down, tempting him with tasty titbits which 1 supplied, but there was no response. Two of them decided to climb the tree, but the monkey snapped and snarled at them so viciously, they were forced to retire. The afternoon wore on and he still sat up there defying us all. Finally, Peter had to say:

"I'm afraid I'll have to shoot him. We can't leave him loose like this, he is too dangerous."

We were all distressed, but we felt that it was true.

"Well I can't bear to look." I said. "I'm going inside."

The girls gladly accompanied me.

Peter, who was an excellent shot, fired twice and hit the monkey each time in the correct places, but he did not die. He screamed and yelled, and screamed again as he clung to the branches. We all turned pale at the sound. Peter stood there, uncertain as to what had happened. He fired again, the screaming went on. He came into the house looking even paler and more shaken than us, saying,

"My God! What's wrong? He just won't die."

At that moment a friend of ours arrived on the scene. We explained what was happening and he asked;

"Would you like me to fire one more shot?"

Peter nodded, but as Jerry fired, to our great relief, the monkey was already falling from the tree. It was unbelievable how long he had hung on after seeing where the bullets had entered. What a miserable affair it was, and how determined we were, including Peter, not to have any further dealings with monkeys.

The days went on very pleasantly. The big house was almost ready for us to move in and so we had quite a lot on our minds. Peter, as usual, was very busy at work. As he arrived home one evening, John came to the door in an agitated and nervous manner to ask if the bwana could please take him into Nairobi to catch the 9pm bus to Kakamega. It was very urgent he said; he had received a message to say his wife was very ill. Although we knew many servants came along with these stories of illness and death in the family when they fancied a holiday, we believed John as he had never tried to deceive us before. So, although Peter was very tired, he agreed to take him the twelve miles back into town.

After the evening meal, the two younger girls went off to bed, Maureen went out with a friend and Peter departed with John; I sat down to relax. Sacunda, the only servant on duty, cleared up and then came as usual to respectfully bid me good night. I heard him lock the door and go off down the garden path to his quarters. All was quiet and still, and then suddenly I became aware of loud voices addressing Sacunda. I stole to the kitchen window to listen. What on earth was going on out there? I now heard Sacunda shouting in reply:

"Kifungua. Kifungua gani?" (Key, what key?) Later I knew Sacunda's shouting had been for my benefit.

"Kifungua ya nyumba," a voice was answering. (The house key.)

"I have no key," shouted Sacunda. Of course I knew he did have the key! There was a lot of mumbling but I distinctly heard one voice saying,

"Come on old man. We don't want to hurt you, but we want the key. We are going in there to kill the memsahib and her children. The day of the white man here is over. Come on now."

I now recognised the voice as belonging to one of the building labourers.

"My God", I trembled, "they must be drunk", but I also realised they meant what they said. I could hear the sounds of struggling. Dashing to the girls' bedroom, I found them both fast asleep.

"Oh dear, it will take ages to wake and dress them", l thought, "I must do something quickly." I knew that there was not much time as I was sure they would soon overpower Sacunda and find the key. Mr. O'Rourke was away so there was no help at that side. We had no telephone in the small house. I rushed back and out of the side door, crept up the verandah steps silently and then flew for my life across the road and over the five acre plot to Frank Bailey's house.

"Thank God he's in," I breathed as I saw the light. My heart almost burst as it thumped in terror.

"Oh Frank," I gasped as I banged on the door, "Oh please come and help me quickly, quickly. There are some Africans trying to get into our house to kill me and the girls. Peter is out and I am so afraid. Please hurry for they are fighting to get the key off Sacunda and then they will get in to the girls who are asleep. I have escaped by the side door."

"There, there now", he calmly surveyed me, assessing the situation as he quickly gathered up his gun, torch and a huge rungu (club).

"Now you just sit there and ring the police post. Tell them to come at once. Don't you worry, we'll soon sort this out."

He shot off through the open doorway and although a big man, he was away and out of sight in a flash. I rang the police and luckily the inspector was in.

"We'll be there in five minutes," he comforted as he banged down the phone.

My legs trembled as I returned home; I couldn't bear to face what might have happened in my absence, but thankfully I could hear Frank's voice calmly speaking to Sacunda. I saw lanterns held by some of our own staff as I walked down the path. As he saw me coming Frank shouted,

"It's alright now, don't worry, all's well."

Lying unconscious on the ground were two building labourers. The police arrived at the same time, so I stayed and talked to them and to ask Sacunda if he was alright. Frank replied,

"Well, he's very much alright now, but he has had a terrific fight protecting you damsels in distress. He was so busy fighting these two blighters they never even heard me creeping up on them, so I was able to smartly lay them both out with the rungu. What a tough old chap he is, and he still has your key safe and sound. The noise finally woke your other staff too and they dashed out to the rescue."

The two 'blighters' were now coming round. The police took over and I left Frank to explain the situation to them whilst I took Sacunda inside. We went to the girls' bedroom to see what state they might be in, but incredibly found they were still asleep, so they never knew any fear. Gratefully, we gently closed the bedroom door behind us.

Surprisingly, Sacunda was not seriously hurt except for bruising and a few small cuts which I dressed. I already knew that Africans did not appear to suffer from too much shock in affrays of this nature, but nevertheless I was very concerned for his well-being. I thanked and praised him for his wonderful tenacity and caring, but he was very modest about what he had done. All he kept repeating was,

"Watu mbaya memsahib, watu mbaya." (Bad men, bad men, memsahib.)

I had always admired him, but now I treasured him for he and Frank I'm sure had saved our lives.

The police inspector and his two askaris took away the two men to lock them up for the night saying they would return in the morning to take a statement. Peter and Maureen on return could hardly believe what had happened in the short time they had been away and were very shocked. We all realised that things were not as 'safe' in Kenya as we had been lulled into believing and that greater security precautions would have to be taken in future.

The two men were charged and put in prison, but not for a very long period as they had not actually entered the house to attack us and Sacunda was not seriously hurt. However, the inspector told me that he had managed to have them banned from entering the Nairobi area at any time in the future; they would immediately be arrested if they did so. It was surprising to find they were not Kikuyus, but members of a very small up-country tribe which disturbed us all as we thought they would not have been contaminated by the evil influences of the past few years.

John returned a few days later and showed no surprise or concern when Sacunda told him of the event. It was not long, however, before he shamefacedly informed me that the two men had threatened him in the afternoon of that awful day, asking him if Sacunda kept the house key at night. They also told him of their plan to kill us all and said if he told anyone they would kill him too. He said he couldn't bear to stay to see what happened, so he had made up the story of going home to his sick wife and asked the bwana to take him to town to escape. How can one understand why he did not tell Peter when he was safely on his way to town? The fact is that John would have been terrified by the intimidation of the two Africans as I well knew, so I forgave him. Intimidation has always been rife in African society and still is today. Threats to the recipient may include his whole family and this he accepts and solemnly believes. An example is the frightening necklacing in South Africa.

CHAPTER SIXTEEN

CHANGING YEARS

Despite our full programme during these days, we managed to make several visits up-country to visit friends. One such visit was to the Bayers, Diana Johnstone's parents, at Njoro. Maureen by now had acquired a car of her own, so proudly offered to drive us up there for the day. All went well as we crossed the Rift Valley, passed through Nakuru, and climbed the hills to the small township of Njoro, when as we drove along the main street, the astonishing sight of a very amorous donkey chasing the female object of his desire met our eyes. The female made straight for our vehicle, banging into the side of it, and jolting us to a hasty halt. Incredibly, the amorous one, not in the slightest deterred in his intent, carried on with his love-making by the car, completely disinterested in any audience, and only moved away later at his leisure.

A large group of Africans had gathered at the scene, being highly delighted by this free and amusing entertainment in the main street on a Sunday morning. They had roared with laughter, but now it was all over, they were concerned and helpful regarding our plight. We found the car badly dented with both doors jammed and poor Maureen was most distressed to find her possession in such a state. She was also very angry as she asked the Africans who the donkeys belonged to. They were all very eager to inform, so we guessed he was not a very popular man. Luckily there was no mechanical damage, so we drove to the police station followed by the crowd, rather like the Pied Piper. The Inspector listened very seriously, although he must have thought the whole thing very humorous. However, he was also relieved to find we were all safe and unharmed by the event. As the owner of the vehicle, Maureen had to fill out the accident form. When it came to the question 'Cause of Accident...' she looked up enquiringly, not without some embarrassment. The Inspector said, with a very straight face,

"I think you can write 'Act of God' in there dear!" as he turned to wink at us.

Of course, there was no hope of receiving any financial assistance towards repairing the car. The most we could hope for was that the donkeys found a new love nest in future where they could not play havoc with other inoffensive motorists' vehicles.

On arrival at our host's home we needed a refreshing drink to get over this shock, which the Bayers were quick to provide and, of course, by this time we saw the funny side of the amazing fiasco and roared with laughter too.

The Bayers had a lovely home on a hillside surrounded by the usual lawns, shrubs and flower beds. They also grew strawberries, commercially, so each day in the season there was great activity to get them picked, packed and down to the railway station in time to catch the afternoon train to Nairobi. Mrs. Bayer was also a great horsewoman, keeping a few ponies for her riding school, so was a very busy lady.

After a very enjoyable day, as we prepared to leave in our battered vehicle, Mrs. Bayer, who was a very persuasive friend, manoeuvred us into taking three baby goats back with us, pets for the girls as she put it. How could we refuse! The girls wanted them, they were pathetically appealing at that age and their names were Gina, Jonquil and Bella. So into the car they came, one on my knee and one each for Val and Elaine. Maureen still insisted on driving us back. What a ride! Our passengers were timid, frightened and very restless. In their anxiety they spent pennies of both varieties endlessly all the way home; the stench in the car increased accordingly. We were more than thankful to relinquish the job of nursemaid when we arrived at our home, where we threw off clothing and had a quick shower. Their little plaintive bleats soon recalled us to fix up a bed for them in an outhouse and get them settled for the night.

Gina, Jonquil and Bella very quickly made themselves at home, roaming on the hillside, round certain areas of the grounds, and if allowed, a quick visit in the house. The girls grew very fond of them as they were so tame, coming when called and liking nothing better than an affectionate hug from their respective owners. However, they grew at an alarming rate and some of their more mischievous antics had to be curtailed. Chewing clothes on the line on washdays did not amuse Sacunda as grumblingly he propped the line higher and higher. We lost a good part of our wardrobes during this period!

That year we had a very sad Christmas, for on Christmas morning when we went to let them out of their house they were not there. They could not have got out themselves and our staff were convinced that they had been stolen during the night. When they suggested that perhaps someone had fancied them for their Christmas dinner, we were upset and appalled. What a miserable way to end their lives. They were such bright and interesting little friends.

Since the scare with the African building labourers we had become much more cautious regarding personal safety. Peter had erected many outside lights for use at night around the two houses and grounds. We never left anyone alone in the house after dark. There seemed to be a more restless atmosphere in the city, and the men noticed a drop off in sales at work. Belgium was preparing to give the Congo its independence. The winds of change were coming but we could not believe that things would alter in Kenya.

We moved over into the big house and rented out the small one to a friend. For a time we were happy setting things straight, having a house warming party, inviting friends to stay with us; in fact a time when we felt a great sense of achievement, along with the added warmth and pleasure of sharing things with the wide circle of friends we had come to know in Kenya, and whose friendship we valued deeply.

However, it was not to last. Peter became increasingly morose about the economical state of Kenya. His company was losing business and Head Office in England was anxious. They tendered for work in Uganda and other areas, even joined forces with a road building company. Some of the staff were transferred to Uganda. Things gradually worsened as the days went by and eventually the company decided to close its Nairobi office. This was a time of great anxiety for us as there was no hope of Peter securing another post, so he decided to open his own small business. He employed some of the Sikhs from the old firm and I offered to help in the office. It started off quite well with friendly architects giving him work whenever possible. Just when we thought we could survive, Belgium gave the Congo an abrupt independence for which the Congolese people were not ready.

The time of terror, rioting and bloodshed that followed in the Congo had a devastating effect on East Africa. Belgians fled for their lives through our territories to reach the port of Mombasa. It was a pitiful sight to see them selling their cars, and any small possessions they had had time to load up, to realise their fares back to Belgium by boat. I watched them from my office window, their sad faces full of despair. Some of them had nothing; some had watched their nearest and dearest ones being slaughtered in the mad rampage which was taking place.

Following this upsetting period many Europeans commenced to leave Kenya. There was a strong rumour that Jomo Kenyatta would soon be released from prison, and a strong undercurrent amongst the natives that if the Congo could achieve independence, then so could Kenya. They looked to Kenyatta for leadership. Kenya experienced a bad recession which affected all races. Uganda was also preparing for independence which did not improve the situation. Still we were assured that Kenya would remain a British Colony.

Peter became more despondent as work declined daily. People leaving the country left without paying for completed jobs. Our financial situation was becoming desperate.

"We had better sell the property, if we can," Peter said one day.

I was shocked. Our lovely home for which we had worked so hard and into which we had put so much care and thought.

"I'm afraid that if we don't sell it now, we may end up like so many people, with nothing. Things are really bad you know. Come with me and I'll show you what I mean," he went on.

He took me on a tour of the Nairobi suburbs; I could not believe what I saw - so many deserted houses, just abandoned and now pillaged. The owners had not been able to sell or rent them and had just left. They already appeared dilapidated in their damaged state combined with overgrown gardens.

I panicked and agreed that we should try to salvage what we could, if only we could find a purchaser. We were lucky; it was such a lovely place we managed to sell it, but the heartbreak of leaving it was hard to bear. What a sense of loss we felt, only followed by the realisation that we must also close the business as trade was completely dead.

We talked of returning to England, but despite all, Peter was confident that if we could sit things out, the situation would improve. He loved the place and never at any time would he agree to leave. Fortunately, he was offered a temporary post in Mombasa looking after a friend's business whilst he went off to search the world for a new place to live. This period was to last four months which gave us a chance to draw breath.

Thank goodness it proved to be a peaceful interlude. We rented a property in Likoni on the edge of the Mombasa harbour channel. Maureen stayed on in Nairobi still working for Armand Denis. Valerie and Elaine transferred to the Loreto Convent in Mombasa and so we arranged some kind of order in our lives.

The coast had always been a world apart and so it still was. The European population was either retired people or government servants in 'safe' positions, the rest being holidaymakers, so they were not feeling the same apprehension as the up-country folk. We were able to relax a little and tried to enjoy each day as much as possible. Social life was still good. A pleasant meeting place was the Whitesands Hotel at Bamburi Beach where we spent many happy weekends, in a homely atmosphere. Although not many people were spending money on a coast holiday, the owners still coped with the patronage of the local people for meals and a few drinks at the bar. Peter gladly helped out on any engineering or electrical faults at the hotel, and in exchange we would be treated to a superb meal!

We also seized the opportunity of exploring the coastal area more thoroughly, especially south of Mombasa which we had not seen much of hitherto, and also other Arabic and Indian buildings in Mombasa itself. Our house was a pleasant white walled bungalow with a large arched verandah where we could sit and watch the cargo and passenger ships sailing in and out of the harbour, accompanied by a small pilot vessel. There was quite a lot of traffic, so according to the tides we were able to enjoy this, to us, novel spectacle at all hours of the day or night. We never grew tired of imagining where they had all come from, or where they were all going on departure. Their hootings were pleasant music to our ears.

Sadly despite malarial precautions, Valerie went down with the dreaded fever. She soon recovered after a few days in bed, but it is a most unpleasant illness. Elaine too, picked up undulant fever which is very debilitating; still despite all, they both enjoyed the change in Mombasa and were happy at the new school.

One thing we discovered was that living and working in Mombasa was not so pleasant as the 'Robinson Crusoe' existence on the beaches during holiday periods. The humidity of the rainy seasons and the excessive heat of December, January and February were extremely tedious to bear. Maureen came down to visit us several times as did Nairobi friends, all confirming that things in the capital city were still very difficult. So, when the time came for us to return, it was with a great degree of apprehension.

CHAPTER SEVENTEEN

HARD TIMES

A kindly providence was to take care of us almost immediately on reaching Nairobi. We were able to rent a house not far from our old home. Peter succeeded in obtaining a post, albeit not well paid, and I was fortunate to find an interesting job at the small light aircraft airport not far from where we lived. This company was a subsidiary of British United Airways and specialised in crop spraying. The girls returned to their beloved school, Maureen was glad to be back at home and thus we hoped to sit out Kenya's depressed period.

Things went quite well, but the uncertainty of the situation we were in was always there. The Europeans felt they dared not fully trust the British Government's promise that it would never relinquish Kenya, as they watched the changing scene. More and more people were leaving; others like Peter were still optimistic.

The turmoil in the Congo continued. Tshombe's government was advertising in the Kenya newspapers for mercenaries, and several soldiers of fortune decided to pay a visit there where looting was a lucrative return for the adventurous. A friend of ours went through a bad time as a result of this. He was approached in Nairobi by one of these adventurers who asked him if he would like to buy some cheap diamonds. Charles could not resist a peep at the jewels although he had no intention of buying them. He was holding the wallet when a police car came alongside, two men jumped out and promptly arrested Charles, whilst the real culprit dashed away down a convenient alley. The Kenya police were very much alive to the situation and were on constant watch for these undesirable characters. Charles spent a miserable few days in jail, until a good lawyer finally convinced the authorities that he was not a member of the gang which had now been rounded up. Other folk, who were prepared to take the risk, also visited the Congo to pick up expensive cars or trucks, which in some cases, were just there for the taking.

Frank Bailey was depressed. Two of his houses were empty which meant a considerably reduced income, plus the added worry of vandalism. He joked, however, that he was now hoping to sell a little insurance in order to exist. Peter decided to help by offering to take out a further small life policy. Of course, this required a medical check up for which he visited the insurance company's doctor. We thought no more of it until a few days later a very anxious looking Frank informed us that Peter's application had been turned down for health reasons. We couldn't believe it! He had not been feeling ill, there were no visible signs of anything wrong; what could it be?

"You'd better see your own doctor, Peter," Frank worriedly advised.

Peter laughed and said it couldn't be anything fatal or he would be the first one to feel it. Perhaps it was a mistake. Secretly I was alarmed so made sure that he quickly visited the doctor. Very high blood pressure readings were discovered and after several visits hypertension and possible arteriosclerosis were diagnosed. What a blow we received as this condition was then a very serious affair. It was another case of the silent killer for Peter said he had no idea that anything was wrong. He was put on a course of experimental tablets, but suffered greatly for several months when these had adverse effects. The fluid balance of his body was greatly disturbed and in turn he had water on the elbows, pneumonia, followed by pleurisy twice. Eventually, however, the right dosage was found and the blood pressure readings became more acceptable. I read up all the medical information I could lay my hands on and knew there was no escape from the seriousness of his condition and that he would be on medication for the rest of his life. I never let him see how worried I was, or how I turned cold when sometimes he would reluctantly say he did not feel well.

It seemed to be our bad luck period as I awoke one morning to more disaster. As I sat drinking my early morning cup of tea, I turned as usual to admire a large poinsettia shrub outside the bedroom window which at the time was a mass of glorious bright red blooms. I thought they were not so vivid today, so blinked and looked again; there was no change. Some natural intuition always warns of things wrong with the human body I believe, for automatically I closed one eye and to my dismay I found I could not see anything. Panicking, I rapidly closed it and tried with the other one which was thankfully normal. Experimenting with each eye I had to admit to myself that one eye was definitely blind. I was frightened, wondering what it could be; was it a temporary nervous blindness perhaps from strain, maybe it would disappear in a day or two I consoled myself. I kept the knowledge to myself for a couple of days, but then firmly went to seek assistance. A friendly optometrist looked in my eyes after which he silently left the room. On return he told me that I was to go straight to the hospital where the eye specialist would see me immediately. I was not seriously worried as I drove to the hospital. The specialist put drops in both my eyes after which he carried out a prolonged examination. I could not see at all now, owing to the drops, and from the darkness I heard him ask,

"Have you just been seriously ill, Mrs. Ellis?"

"No," I replied.

"That's very odd," he mused, and then went on, "I think you have picked up some kind of virus. We'll have to take some blood tests and in the meantime I'll give you four different kinds of drugs to see if we can hit the right one to clear it up."

He explained that the blood would be sent to America as there were no facilities in Nairobi for detecting the kind of infection he thought I had. He did not tell me at that stage that people with this infection usually had a very high fever first and then went blind in one eye.

"Now you go home and rest," he advised. "Is there anyone with you?"

"No," I replied in some alarm as I knew I could not see to drive the car.

"Those drops will affect your vision for quite a while before they wear off, but the sight will come back in your good eye," he consoled. "Now, who can I ring up to come and collect you?"

And so the family had to be informed just when I did not want them to have further worry. They were shocked and concerned at this event. I had been too stunned myself to ask the specialist if I would regain the sight of my eye. I grumbled at the enforced resting period but after two or three days I was glad to collapse into my bed with the worst fever I had ever had in my life. With a temperature of 104° which refused to come down, the family doctor visited to say it might be tick typhus, malaria, anything but what it finally turned out to be which was toxoplasmosis, picked up from some animal, most likely a cat or dog. As we had a cat who had recently developed a blind eye we decided he must be the culprit. I never recovered the sight in that eye but was fortunate to have a little blurred and distorted vision which has saved me from looking blind and really I have always managed to cope very well with one eye. My workmates were marvellous to me during this unhappy period, kind and helpful, covering my duties until I could return to the office.

By this time, Valerie was nearing the end of her school days. How quickly the girls seemed to be growing up. Maureen was bringing home a string of boyfriends, some lasting a very short time, others for much longer periods. Valerie was offered a post in the same company as myself, but in a new department set up for the collection of vervet monkeys. These were later transported by air to laboratories in Germany, England and America to supply poliomyelitis vaccine. It was quite an involved business, with trappers in Tanzania who caught the monkeys by means of large nets thrown over trees at early dawn whilst the monkeys were still drowsy. The next step was not so easy as they were transferred into canvas sacks with handles, which were hung on rods in Oxford aircraft, for their onward journey to Nairobi. This was the most humane way of carrying them so they did not injure themselves in their frantic efforts to escape. In Nairobi they were again transferred into individual cages in a large hangar where they were inspected by a veterinary surgeon. They had to be given a clean bill of health followed by a three week quarantine period before going on to their final destination. Perhaps a gruesome kind of business until one thought how this was helping to eradicate a dreadful affliction of the human race. Valerie's duties lay only in the office so she did not come into contact with the vervets.

We had a very friendly group of pilots, some being ex-Squadron Leaders from World War II - great characters in their own way. One of them was very fond of shooting and fishing, so when he was away on crop spraying trips which were made at the crack of dawn, he would squeeze in some trout fishing afterwards. Arriving back at the

Nairobi office he would dash into the little kitchen where he had installed a hot plate, pop the trout in a buttered cooking dish, cook them to perfection and supply us all with a gourmet lunch. How delicious they were! Other times he would turn up with a sack of pheasants, ducks and geese which he would generously share out. At the Annual Air Rally we felt great pride when our pilots put on a spectacular show.

For three months each year they left us for the spraying of cotton in the Sudan. This was a very taxing period for them with a large acreage to cover in a very short time. They lived in spartan quarters and suffered greatly from eating and drinking questionable food and water. One of them swore he only ate hard boiled eggs and bananas during his stay there to try and avoid the dreaded dysentery. When they reached Entebbe on their way back to Nairobi at the end of the season, Air Traffic Control would transfer their radio calls through to our switchboard. We were as excited to receive these as they were to be returning home and some of the conversations were hilarious.

Sadly, we lost a young Scandinavian pilot on one of these contracts who was only twenty four years of age. Apparently he flew off near dusk one day to inspect the area for the next day's spraying. A very large bird had hit his aircraft which then crashed; he was killed instantly. His body was sent down to Nairobi and how desolate we all felt attending his funeral; how concerned for his broken hearted parents.

The political situation in the country was still very unsettled. We were stunned and could not believe it had happened when the rumour regarding Jomo Kenyatta's release from prison became reality in 1961. His arrival in Nairobi was something to behold! Thousands of Africans lined the streets to cheer and support him. After this, political meetings were held at various venues each weekend with Jomo Kenyatta as chief speaker. A brilliant young Jaluo, named Tom Mboya, was also very prominent at these meetings, who, although not a Kikuyu, strongly and loyally supported Jomo Kenyatta in his fight for Kenya's Independence.

Peter's company, looking for further trade, promoted him to Sales Manager East Africa, which meant that he was involved in trips to Uganda for periods of two or three weeks at a time. I worried about his health when he was away, and he too worried about us being left in an isolated country area, as attacks were now being made on Europeans. These were usually robberies at night but if any Europeans happened to awake, then it was certain that violence would ensue. So off we went again to live in the Hill district of Nairobi in a lovely old stone house with a terraced garden. The company gave us a night watchman to guard us and our possessions when he was away. Poor man! He was so old and pathetically weak and had a dreadful cough. At night, he would sit on our verandah steps near my bedroom window, dozing off or incessantly coughing, a cough reminiscent of the song of India which kept me constantly awake. Eventually, in desperation, I had to ask the company to remove him, especially as I would not have given much for our chances with him as our sole saviour.

Frank Bailey paid us a further visit; he had come to say good-bye. We couldn't believe that Frank was throwing in the towel and really leaving Kenya for good for he loved the place. However, with his third house now standing empty, and deprived of any income, how could he stay. Luckily he managed to sell the three houses for pathetically small amounts to young people who still had faith in Kenya's future, but he had to let them go with no deposit and the amount payable over five years. Frank did not want to go, it broke his heart, and we did not wish to lose such a good friend, but sadly we had to wish him 'Bon Voyage'.

He drove an old Wolseley car up through Kenya and Uganda where it was loaded onto a Nile steamer at Juba on which he travelled up through Egypt. Then he motored along the coast of North Africa, crossed the Straits of Gibraltar, followed by more motoring through Spain and France and so reached the shores of the English Channel.

Writing to us later, he was proud to relate that he had no trouble with the car except for one puncture which occurred right outside a garage in Spain! The car was ancient and he never even had it serviced before leaving Kenya so we could hardly believe his luck. However, he had succumbed to malaria on the Nile steamer, but recovered sufficiently to enjoy the ride across North Africa which he had found very interesting and very beautiful in parts. He sounded depressed with the grey days of England and was missing the sunshine and wide open spaces. In later years he left England and went to live in New

Zealand.

Frank bequeathed his hens to us. However, Blondie fretted and was not at all happy. We were no substitute for her beloved Frank. One morning the cook told us that all the hens had been stolen during the night, so we never knew what end she came to experience. We could not bear to tell Frank the news. These kind of happenings became all too frequent. The Africans in the city were restless and there was an air of disinterest in working areas. Our personal safety and tightening up on security were the things foremost in our thoughts.

At this time I lost some faith in John, our head gardener. For some time I had heard a child crying in the servants' quarters at night. It was a cry of pain and no one seemed to be comforting the child. I decided it was time I investigated and to my horror I found John's three year old daughter in a dreadful condition. Her small legs were covered with scabies sores of such long standing that the flesh of her legs was appalling to behold. I was speechless and then very angry. I took her to the house and then down to hospital for treatment. When she came home I personally fed her daily until she was well. I got no explanation from John for this terrible cruelty. The only thing I felt might have some connection was the fact that he had produced a new wife and perhaps she was a jealous culprit. However, I made sure there was no repeat performance of this cruelty which was unusual for, in the main, Africans are very fond of their children.

CHAPTER EIGHTEEN

UGANDA

The African population were now very sure that they were on the way to Independence, but Kenya still remained in its recessed state thus affecting all races economically. However, the African young felt excited and stimulated; their elders only a worried caution. Our African staff showed no change in their relationship with us, but we could sense their anxiety and a certain awakening to the fact that the future held a change in their circumstances.

To stimulate further trade, Peter was asked to set up a new company in Kampala, the capital city of Uganda, which would take at least six weeks. Possibly he was not feeling too well at this time for he said he would like me to go with him. This, of course, meant leaving the girls and my job which caused me agonies of indecision. I was worried for the girls' welfare, but when a young English couple we knew agreed to come and live in the house for this period I agreed to go. Sacunda, Andrea and John would also be there to care for them so my fears were reduced.

It was a long trip by car. As we journeyed along I felt sad and restless and could not enjoy the beauty of the familiar countryside. We decided to spend the night at the Farm Hotel, beyond Nakuru, as we had not left home until late afternoon. Nostalgia for other days hit me as I watched the African staff lighting huge log fires in the lounge and dining room. We were the only guests and the Africans seemed depressed and uncomfortable. I remembered it only as a place full of happy, laughing holidaymakers.

Next morning we reached Eldoret, full of memories of Maureen's school days, then on to Tororo and Jinja in Uganda which I had never seen. At Jinja I was escorted to the place where a plaque informs one that here on the 28th July 1862, the explorer Speke discovered the source of the River Nile. We spent a further night with friends in Jinja who had a house by the side of the lake. It was a lovely home with large shady verandahs. They told us that hippos came out of the lake at night to cavort on the grass lawns causing a great deal of damage. There did not seem to be a great deal of social life for them and I wondered if they really liked living there. There was a large army barracks, a tobacco factory, where our friend worked, and very little else. However, they did get home leave to England each year due to the trying climate and their house was exceedingly comfortable.

As we neared Kampala the following day, we passed large sugar plantations owned by the Mehta and Madhvani Groups. Uganda was very warm and humid which I found rather unpleasant, but it was lush and green with very fertile soil. The local African women walking by the roadside were more colourfully attired than their Kenya counterparts in their long traditional dresses with matching head-dresses.

Peter took me to a small hotel on the outskirts of Kampala which he thought I would prefer rather than the inner city ones. We settled into a rather bleak bedroom with a cement floor which had very old and uncomfortable furniture, but at least we had a bathroom, and there was a swimming pool in the grounds. The staff were friendly and the food plain but good, so I was not unhappy. Next morning I was taken on a tour of Kampala which was smaller than Nairobi. I found a difference in the atmosphere, the people, the vegetation and the climate. Kampala, like Rome, is situated on seven hills, a very attractive setting. The centre of the city was dominated by Parliament Buildings. The Law Courts were set in beautiful landscaped gardens; on top of one hill was the huge Catholic Cathedral, a spectacular landmark. There was a large hospital, the Grand Hotel and streets of Indian shops and eating houses. It all looked very pleasant in the morning sunshine. Suburbs of elegant homes were established on other hills. I experienced visiting my very first supermarket in one area which, to me, at that time, was quite a novelty.

It was a comfortable feeling to know that we had two lots of friends in Uganda, one family in Kampala and the other in Entebbe. I was saved by them from a rather boring period, for when Peter drove away each day I found it difficult to fill in time at the small hotel.

I read or fretted for my home and the girls in Nairobi. It was too hot to visit town often as this entailed waiting around for Peter to pick me up, so I was always delighted when Mabs called to ask me out for the day. At weekends we drove out to Entebbe to spend time with Pat and Peter. Peter was an air traffic control officer at the small airport and their home was situated near the lake. We were staggered by the size of Lake Victoria which they informed us covered more than 13,000 square miles. Entebbe was a small place, the residents being chiefly civil servants. Beautiful Government House was the main feature with the other housing scattered around in pleasant, shady avenues. There was an hotel which was chiefly used by airline staff for their rest periods. Huge lawns and a golf course swept back from the lake and another attraction was a miniature zoo.

We enjoyed these interludes; our only complaint being about mosquitoes which plagued one to death. They were enormous compared with the few we had in Nairobi and I asked how they coped with them. Pat said the mosquitoes were not the main problem but the lake flies which came over in clouds. They were minute so could squeeze through the wire mesh of the screens on doors and windows and become a menace. I soon discovered that Uganda had more large and small insects than I was ever likely to see again. When Winston Churchill visited Entebbe in 1911 he called it a poisoned paradise because of sleeping sickness.

We had already become aware that Uganda was almost as politically unsettled as Kenya, despite having achieved Independence. The military were everywhere. It was the old story of tribal differences still unsolved, plus the added burden of the Kabaka's domain and in the areas of old kingdoms which had been ruled separately for centuries. We drove past the Kabaka's palace one day which had a silver dome and guards outside the sentry boxes at the gates. It had a simple dignity. Sadly, it was soon to be burned to the ground.

Peter's six weeks unfortunately became six months as there was so much to organise. The new company was a subsidiary of the Mehta millionaire group and they had asked specially for him to stay on.

"Oh no!" I pleaded. Visions of six months in the hotel were too much for me to contemplate.

I dare not suggest going home and leaving him alone as I knew he was not well. Mabs saved the day for us. She was the housing officer for Shell Company in Kampala and so was able to offer us one of their vacant furnished houses on Mbuyu Hill, as by a lucky coincidence, one of their staff members had just gone off on six months leave. Shell did not care for their houses to stand empty in this unsettled land and so for a nominal rent we acquired a beautiful home which had a terraced garden and a magnificent view of Lake Victoria from the verandah. By coincidence too, Elaine's school days were over, so the three girls made a trip to Kampala in Maureen's car for a short holiday. They brought Andrea who would stay to help in the house, and Elaine also stayed on. The other two were quite happy about returning to their posts in Nairobi and said they had not had any security problems, so once again we seemed to have organised the situation into something bearable.

We had a good holiday with the girls, showing them around and visiting Entebbe. One Sunday we made a visit to Masaka, which is about 100 miles south west of Kampala, exploring this new area of Uganda along the way. We found the countryside very fertile with many green hills and valleys. The little town was smart and clean with lots of shady trees and a modern hotel where we lunched. An unusual modern Catholic Cathedral caught our interest; we called in and admired the internal architecture and the spiritual atmosphere created by the sun shining through the stained glass windows, so placed to catch the rays, which formed rainbow patterns on the walls, floor and altar. There were schools and playing fields, where as usual, happy children ran, laughed and played. Walking down the main street we met a group of Chinese in Mao uniforms, a strange sight then in Africa, and we wondered what they could be doing there where they seemed so out of place. Today I look back on peaceful Masaka and Entebbe as they were then. Later they were to become scenes of terror in the days when Idi Amin came to power in Uganda.

We became quite fond of our new home which was large and modern. Andrea coped very well with the household chores and the Shell company gardener kept the grounds spick and span. Elaine decided to take a shorthand and typing course to fill in the time and so the days went by. Being so close to the lake did mean that we suffered from the electric air pressures which built up during the day over the water until the atmosphere became almost unbearable. At that time of the year one could set the clock for a fantastic thunderstorm around 4pm after which the rest of the day was cooler and very pleasant. I would eagerly await its arrival and usually sat on the verandah watching the terrific downpour and the fireworks display of lightning over the lake which was a wonderful revelation, though somewhat frightening.

We were invited, with Peter, to visit the Mehta compound on the Jinja road, where the main house was situated on top of the hill like a huge pink icing sugar castle. There was evidence of great wealth with many other family homes spreading down the hillside. The huge sugar cane plantations, which were responsible for the initial wealth, stretched further than the eye could see in all directions. We toured the factories and met many of the family members who all worked hard in this massive empire, for they had many more interests than the sugar industry. We knew their ancestor had arrived from India with very few assets, working his way up from Mombasa to Uganda, where he traded and gradually built up a prosperous company; they had never looked back. Idi Amin was later to evict the Asians from Uganda, including the Mehta and Madhvani families, and take over their possessions. Fate is a fickle master!

Peter casually mentioned one day that he had advertised for a secretary to clear up all the paperwork now being created. The Uganda Government's policy after Independence was for employers to take on as many Africans as possible, but this was not always easy due to their lack of training and experience at that time. Not many African girls had mastered the intricacies of shorthand and typing so we were surprised when he came home a few days later to say he had not had any difficulty in choosing an African girl for the post. He said she spoke perfect English, could spell correctly, knew shorthand and typed beautifully. Some time later he casually mentioned that she was a marvel at work and appeared to have a chauffeur boy friend who dropped her off at the office each morning from a large Mercedes car. A little worriedly, he wondered if the boy would get into trouble if his employer found out that he was driving her around. Time passed on until again he talked of her, saying that she had invited him, along with his family, to her twenty first birthday party on the coming Saturday. Today that would not have posed a problem, but at that time it did a little. We did not know what kind of a party it would be or what food we might be expected to eat or what area we might have to visit at night in those troubled times. So we compromised, not wishing to appear discourteous, and agreed to go just for an hour or so, giving the excuse of a previous invitation.

Elaine and I purchased a nice present for her and on the due evening we set out to follow the directions she had drawn for Peter to find her home. This was on Kololo Hill and we were a little puzzled owing to it being a suburb of high quality housing. We found the correct road where there appeared to be great activity and congestion of traffic. The police were there in numbers, waving us on and up the hill past the entrance to a large house at whose gates were sentry boxes with guards. Several cars were entering the driveway and Peter remarked,

"Someone else is having a party tonight too!"

As we reached the summit we realised that we must have passed the number we were looking for, so round we turned, only to find we were back at the large house and the right number adorned the gatepost! A police officer came over and Peter asked who lived in the house. We were startled to hear the reply,

"The King of Toro, bwana!"

Peter looked at me in astonishment and said,

"Good God! Well I suppose we'd better go in."

At the huge entrance we were greeted by my husband's secretary who was wearing a beautiful evening dress and tiara. She introduced us to several brothers and sisters, one of whom was Princess Elizabeth of Toro who later became a world famous model. We mingled with the other guests as we explored the ground floor of this lovely mansion. In one room a banquet fit for kings, as one might aptly say, was laid out on enormous tables. We were led out to a courtyard at the back which was illuminated by thousands of fairy lights; a full band was playing softly in the background. What a lovely hour we spent there until Kassia approached to softly say,

"What a pity you have to go. I do wish you could only stay."

Very, very reluctantly we had to leave to save face.

As we drove home Peter chuckled,

"Well you'd better treat me with due respect in future. It's not everyone you know who has a Princess for his secretary!"

Time was now passing pleasantly enough apart from two scares with spiders and snakes. Each day I would walk around the terraces collecting a few gardenias which bloomed profusely in this warm, humid environment. Sometimes I would hear a rustle in the rocky banks and knew that it must be a snake, for Mbuyu is known as the hill of snakes. One morning there was a great deal of agitated shouting in the garden. I was called out to find our gardener, along with several other gardeners from neighbours' properties, holding a long pole over which hung a dead 8 foot mamba which they said they had killed in the rockery. I shuddered as I realised how close I had been to death in my daily wanderings for the mamba strikes quicker than the wink of an eye and I could not believe how they had managed to kill it. Now there had to be a big purge for neighbours warned there would be the rest of the mamba family to account for as snakes do not live alone. The fire brigade was called in with their long ladders as trees are a favourite haunt of snakes. Teams of men beat through the surrounding undergrowth and the final toll was 8 dead mambas!

Another evening we were dressing to go out to dinner. Peter was in the bath. Elaine went to her room and then dashed out again looking pale.

"Help!" she shouted. "There's a huge spider on the back of my bedroom door."

"Oh come now," I tried to reassure her, thinking it could only be a house spider as the whole house was screened to keep insects out. We had been used to large spiders for years, most of them harmless, and had become very adept at swatting doubtful ones with a rolled up newspaper or anything handy.

"Just wallop it with something. Come on now, we haven't got much time."

"No fear!" she gasped, "I'm not going back in there. I tell you, it's enormous."

Bravely I flung open the bedroom door and then stopped dead. Gently backing out and feeling very faint, I slammed the door. It was a tarantula! Dad had to come to the rescue from his bath, wrapped only in a large towel. His only weapons were the sweeping brush and mop from the kitchen but he somehow managed to kill it after almost having a heart attack when it started to stalk him.

The same night we had another scare from the military personnel who had a large camp in a meadow at the foot of the hill. As we returned home at midnight two soldiers with rifles stopped us at the entrance to the road which led to the Shell boma. They were not friendly, and although they knew us, asked for identity cards and where we were going. They seemed reluctant to let us drive on and as we were from Kenya finally said that we must produce our passports next day without fail. Fulfilling this obligation, we heard nothing further and wondered why we had been treated so. Later we heard that another couple driving in at night had been shot at; luckily the bullets passing straight through the open windows of the car. After this we did not care to go out at night, and especially so when we heard gunfire on several occasions. We decided they were very trigger happy soldiers and were most relieved to hear a little later that the camp had been moved to another area.

However, we now found that the Army and Police were continually setting up road blocks in Kampala and other outer areas where one could irritatingly be held up for long periods. Distant gunfire became a familiar sound. Elaine had been given a little post in Parliament buildings taking notes for a parliamentary secretary. She was shocked one day to see armed soldiers positioned on all the roofs of surrounding buildings and hoped that she would get home safely. She did, in the event, but paid no further visits to help the secretary.

Each Tuesday, Pat and Peter from Entebbe, visited Kampala to do their weekly grocery shopping. On the way home they would call in for tea and an early sundowner drink. We were surprised one Tuesday to see them arriving at lunch time looking very shaken and upset. They told us the road from Entebbe had been lined with soldiers and civilians who were all throwing huge stones and rocks at passing motorists. They were lucky to be alive as several cars had been hit and people badly injured thus ending up in the ditches. No one was helping them as people dare not stop or they would only suffer the same fate. Now they were extremely worried as to how they could get back to Entebbe for they had left their daughter Judith at school.

We turned on the radio and heard announcements of expected civil war. Peter rang the British High Commission and was told by an officer there that all British subjects must remain indoors and contact them by telephone, if possible, at regular intervals for instructions in case the position became serious. By early evening, we were still advised to remain indoors. Pat and Peter rang their home in Entebbe several times but received no reply. They became more and more concerned as the night wore on. We could not obtain information on the position in Entebbe. Suddenly, our friend Peter, made the decision to drive back, providing there were no road blocks. He was convinced that he could drive without lights and at great speed as he knew every inch of the road. We tried hard to dissuade him, but to no avail. Pat insisted on going with him, much to our horror, and as they drove off we shouted,

"Please ring us the minute you get back. If we don't hear in one hour we will inform the High Commission."

Peter promised to do so and thanked us as away they flew. How glad and relieved we were to hear the phone ring after only half an hour when they let us know that they had found Judith safe with a neighbour. They said that troops were still around and armoured cars were patrolling the streets of Entebbe, but no one had bothered them.

Episodes such as this clouded our last days in Uganda, so we were grateful when the time came for us to motor back to our home in Nairobi. We did not envy our friends who had to remain there under such unpleasant conditions and thought of them often during the following days. It was shortly after we left that the Kabaka's palace was destroyed, but the Kabaka himself was not caught, and managed to escape to London.

In 1971 Idi Amin took over from Milton Obote in Uganda after a so-called bloodless coup, but from then on blood did flow as thousands of Africans died. Many of them were soldiers from rival tribes loyal to Obote who was out of the country at the time of the coup. He went into exile in Tanzania. Others were Christians, including one archbishop, intellectuals and officials he did not trust. People disappeared and were never seen again. The means by which they were exterminated were so shocking that the whole world shuddered.

In 1972 Amin turned on the Asian population of Uganda, some 50,000 strong, using them as an excuse for the country's faltering economy. They were ordered to leave by a certain date. Some were Ugandan citizens, but they were afraid to stay. Those with British passports had to rely on Britain to evacuate them. Those with no papers tried to escape to Kenya and other places. They boarded trains, but soldiers stopped the trains, took their jewels and any other items they had managed to take with them. Many were beaten up and the women taken away and raped. All these Asians had to leave their houses and wealth behind even though they were, in many cases, second or third generation Ugandans.

The lovely little town of Masaka which we had visited during our time in Uganda was the scene for many crimes. One horrifying episode was when the former Mayor was taken from his home by one of Amin's men to the Tropic Inn where we had lunched. Soldiers then took him outside and stripped him naked. They tied his hands and ankles and then castrated him. He was flung into the back of a lorry and driven away, never to be seen again. Local inhabitants witnessed this dreadful act.

The days of Idi Amin are over. Milton Obote regained control of Uganda in the later days of the 70's. Although little news got out to the world at large during his second term as President, it was found later when he was ousted for the second time, that there had been further mass killings.

Let us hope that the present regime can give faith, hope and peace to Uganda.

CHAPTER NINETEEN

INDEPENDENCE YEARS

How good it was to be a whole family again, back in our own home. I had become extremely anxious regarding Peter's health in Uganda; the climate seemed to have an adverse effect on him and he had suffered from many heavy nose bleeds. Another anxiety, of course, had always been there for the two girls in Nairobi as there was still a great deal of violence in Kenya. Maureen's 21st birthday was very near so it was a pleasure to be home in time to give her a birthday party where we were all reunited with our friends. We forgot our cares and danced the night away. Some young British airmen driving past our home heard the music, and politely asked if they could join the party, which caused some jealous competition with the local boys. But it was all great fun, and we have very happy memories of that day.

Maureen had grown up so quickly, and I could not believe that she was 21, and a very accomplished young lady. Often, people who had been to England would excitedly tell her that they had watched the Denis programmes on TV there and had seen her name on the credit lists. She shyly accepted their compliments and wished that we had television in Kenya. How the years had rolled away. Elaine took her first post, and although very young, she was chosen as secretary to the Matron at the Aga Khan Hospital, so was to meet the present Aga Khan who had in 1956, taken over from his grandfather. Val moved to a new field with the 20th Century Fox Films publicity department where she met many famous visiting film stars. We were very proud of them all.

But now the days came when we felt betrayed. The British Government admitted approaching Independence for Kenya. A coalition government would be formed with both European and African Ministers for one year, the foremost of whom would be Jomo Kenyatta. There was a great outcry from the farming community regarding compensation if they had to leave. There were so many magnificent and productive farms which had been brought from barren bush land to their present state by the planning, care and toil of two or three generations. They were assured that they would receive a pay out from the British Government as their farms were gradually taken over by the Africans. Civil servants, too, would receive a golden handshake as they were phased out. However, business people, professionals and retired people were left out in the cold. It would be left to them whether or not they stayed on. Some whites did decide to go. It was said that the Kikuyu had compiled a black list of Europeans who would not be allowed to stay after Independence. It included business managers, farmers, some police and Special Branch officers, people they considered had been anti-Kikuyu. Where possible, the Special Branch warned these people that it would be best to leave in order to evade any danger to their lives. We discussed whether or not we should leave, but Peter's optimistic outlook won the day.

This year of coalition was not an easy one for us, but all went as planned in the political field. A date for Independence was set in 1963. Jomo Kenyatta would be President of Kenya and some Europeans would still be Ministers. As the day approached and preparations were being made for the ceremony, Kenya at last set up its own television service. We watched the proceedings this way in our own lounge. Hundreds of thousands of Africans thronged the arena and the streets of Nairobi. Prince Philip represented the British; as the Union Jack was lowered and the Kenya flag hoisted he asked Jomo Kenyatta if he would like to change his mind as it was not an easy task to run a country! Whilst Kenyatta was imprisoned in Lodwar the British allowed him to have a chief's daughter, Ngina, live with him. She became his third wife. All three of his wives and their families attended the ceremony.

After this affair we all felt the need of a holiday and so we arranged for one at the Mwingo Hotel on the slopes of Kilimanjaro in Tanzania. We happily motored down the familiar road, calling in at our favourite haunts on the way, and reached the attractive, welcoming hotel at dusk. Next morning, the ethereal surroundings of Kilimanjaro made it feel so good to be alive where one experienced this profound closeness to God and nature. We collected a picnic lunch from the hotel staff, intent on spending as much time as possible outdoors, and slowly drove the car up a mountain track. Where it ended a convenient rocky ledge provided a good parking area. From here we climbed down the side of a magnificent valley where waterfalls fell over rocky crags into a crystal clear stream which bubbled along over boulders at the foot of the hill. At a bend in the valley we sat by a quiet pool. The mountain air was invigorating; we felt so well and far from care. What fascination Africa held at such moments. We saw buck wandering through the trees, some of them pausing to drink from the stream, lifting their little heads to listen and sniffing the air. After a lovely day in the valley we retraced our steps up the hillside.

As we reached the car I laid my handbag on the roof as I busily helped to stow away the picnic gear. Suddenly, from nowhere, a group of African children appeared who stood around gazing at us curiously. Gradually overcoming their shyness they began to converse, asking us where we had come from and where we were staying. Some of them were quite delightful and wore the uniform of a Catholic school we had noticed in the trees near the hotel. We became quite engrossed in conversation, but I did notice at one stage that two rougher type youths had joined the group. Very forgetful, when we jumped in the car to drive away, I left my bag on the roof. We heard it fall and stopped immediately to retrieve it, but one of the rough youths beat us to it. He grabbed the bag and made off with his friend at great speed up the mountain, weaving in and out of the trees, sure-footed as a mountain goat. We raced after him, slipping and stumbling in the rough terrain until we were breathless, but he was far away and gone out of sight. Some of the school children followed us showing their indignation that we should have suffered such a loss. One of them said he knew who the youth was and where he lived and that we should go there and talk to his parents.

Bewildered by the occurrence we silently followed them up the mountain, a trip which exhausted us as we must have walked two miles up the steep slope. We came upon a neglected sordid looking hut standing in a clearing where scraggy goats and fowls wandered in a filthy yard. There was no sound from the hut, but eventually a sullen looking woman appeared. When questioned she said she had not seen her son for days. We told her what had happened and that we would have to report the matter to the police as there were things of great value in the bag. She shrugged indifferently and shuffled back into her home. How frustrated we felt. It was a real calamity as the bag contained all the cash to pay for our holiday and hotel bill, as Tanzania at that time, would not accept Kenya cheques.

Disheartened, we returned to the car and then drove on to the local police post to report the affair. They displayed no concern but asked for a statement. I sat with an African officer who prepared to write out the official report. I soon discovered that although he must write this in English, he knew very little spoken or written English. I tried Swahili hoping it would make things easier for him but, of course, it made little difference. He slowly and laboriously scrawled on the paper something which must have been quite indecipherable. After two hours I desperately asked if he would like me to finish it for him. He was furious; his dignity was insulted; he snarled at me and said I was not allowed to write my own report, just sign it! It was dark when he finally allowed us to stagger out of the building. We knew then that there would be no hope of ever seeing the bag again.

At the hotel we talked with the manager about our plight and although extremely sorry for us he could see no way for us to stay on for our holiday and pay later. Luckily Peter just had enough cash in his wallet to pay for the two nights if we left early next morning, plus 30 shillings which would buy sufficient petrol for our return journey home. How disappointed and depressed we all were. I felt desperately guilty about being so careless, thus spoiling what had started out as a wonderful holiday.

Next morning we drove down the hill from the hotel at the foot of which we found a road block manned by two of the Africans from the police post. One of them waved us on and we proceeded across the road to a petrol station to fill up the tank. Imagine our amazement when suddenly the two askaris chased after us waving their rifles and screaming,

"Why did you not stop when we told you to stop?"

"But you never asked us to stop, you waved us on," Peter answered in astonishment.

"How dare you," they ranted, "you must now drive to the police post at once."

"But why?" he demanded. "You know us. We were with you last night reporting the theft of a handbag. Now that we have no money we are returning to our home."

One of them replied, "I have never seen you before."

We looked at each other, feeling very scared, as we had heard stories of Europeans being jailed in Tanzania for imaginary offences, and dreaded what they might be planning for us. Maybe I had offended the policeman more than I had realised the previous evening when I offered to write the report, but I had certainly not intended any derision.

The Officer-in-Charge came out of the police building and asked for our passports. They had been in Peter's suitcase so had survived the robbery. He silently handed them over. The African opened them one by one, curiously turning the pages for what seemed an interminable length of time. I walked a little closer and discovered that he had them upside down! He returned to the building. We were left standing in the morning sun with the two askaris watching our every movement. Nine o'clock, ten o'clock, eleven o'clock went by. The girls climbed into the back seat of the car to escape from the rising temperature. As there was no protest I sat on the front seat with the door open. Peter, however, was not allowed to move. Twelve o'clock came and he whispered,

"My God! This is stupid. I'm going to get us out of here."

He started to walk towards the building but was immediately stopped by the askaris. I turned to the girls anxiously whispering,

"Whatever can we do?"

"Would it help if I pretended to be ill or something?" Maureen whispered back.

I thought that might be a good idea, at least it would create a diversion, so I said,

"Yes, yes! Put on the act of your life. Stagger out of the car and do your best. I will then be able to say we were taking you to the doctor when they stopped us."

Maureen's experience in the film world, plus the fact that she was not feeling well anyway from the combination of heat and anxiety, resulted in a truly star performance. She commenced to moan and groan, waving her arms around in the car, then pushing her sisters aside she slumped out of the door onto the ground. Shakily raising herself in stages she staggered over to a grassy patch where she tried to vomit. She called for me to help her saying that she was in dreadful pain. Doubling herself up and falling to the ground again she writhed in a pretence of great agony. The askaris began to look concerned. They whispered to each other and then one of them went off to the office. Maureen continued with her act; I joined in, shouting to the askari left to help us as my daughter was very ill. The officer-in-charge came out, looking over at us speculatively, and so I accused him of detaining us unnecessarily, and asked why. Could he not see that my daughter was very sick and that we had intended taking her to the doctor at Moshi. He looked disconcerted. Peter took the chance of saying,

"Yes, I shall have something to say about this to Mr... (a high ranking government official in Tanzania whom we had met through business). Now kindly let us proceed on our way."

We couldn't believe it! He handed back our passports and told us to go, but at the last moment belligerently shouted,

"When you have been to the hospital at Moshi you go straight to the Immigration Centre and sign in."

How thankful we were to drive away. We forgot the petrol and filled up in Moshi, then shot off from there like the wind to the Tanzania border at Namanga. Safely through we vowed never to return; we never did! The experience saddened our hearts. I knew then that one day the white man would have no place in Africa and wondered how long we could hope to stay.

It was shortly after this trip that we visited the Aero Club in Nairobi on the occasion of the Annual Air Rally. Some of the African Ministers were there, including Tom Mboya, who presented the prizes.

At the social gathering in the evening, Peter introduced me to

Lawrence Sagini who was Minister for Local Government. He seemed a very nice person who had been at university in America for many years. He came from Kisii near Lake Victoria and was a great friend of Tom Mboya. In the course of conversation he said that he was looking for a personal secretary, preferably English. I thought nothing of it at the time so was astonished a few days later when Peter came home to say that Lawrence Sagini had contacted him to ask if he thought I would be interested in the post. Hannah Stirling, the niece of David Stirling, had been working for him temporarily but now had to leave for England. She also telephoned me to ask me to take the post. She said that I would love working for Mr. Sagini as he was a marvellous person, and that I would be just right for the position.

I was totally unprepared for this kind of offer and felt completely speechless. I didn't know what to think. Secretary in an African Government in Kenya was something I surely could not visualise. Would it be an embarrassment if I did not accept? Would it be an embarrassment if I accepted and hated it and wished to leave? Could I cope with the responsibility? Did I really wish to be part of an African Government in Kenya? What did Peter feel about it? He agreed that he had been surprised at the offer, but that Lawrence was a good person and that if I agreed he would be quite happy for me to work with him. He also said that if we wanted to stay in the country we would have to grow with, and help to build up, a happy multi-racial society. He thought many whites would stay on and that the Indians would not leave. I was not so sure, and much more uncertain about the future, but I dearly loved Kenya. So I took the job and never regretted the action.

I was to spend eighteen months with Lawrence Sagini in the most interesting, stimulating period of my working life, working harder than I had ever done before and enjoying every minute. He had a delightful personality - kind, considerate, humorous, hard working and shrewd in his political career, but also he had an overall love and understanding of the human nature of the white, black and Asian races of Kenya. He was also a very religious man, a devout Catholic. We became firm friends in an easy relationship which reached a stage where we could read each other's minds in both the working and social fields.

At this time two events occurred which also changed our lives.

Maureen went down with amoebic dysentery and had a spell in hospital. The Denis' had arranged to work in America for a while as the new Government rules regarding the making of films in Kenya had caused them some difficulties, and other frustrations, such as the holding up of film at the airport, were hindering their output. So they were going away until Kenya had time to settle down. They had been hopeful of Maureen joining them, but her illness had depressed her and she declined the invitation. Regretfully, they came to the hospital to bid her adieu and this was the end of her association with them. Later, when she was restored to health, she joined Kenya Television Services as their editor.

The second change was moving house once again. The farmer owners of our house on the hill had been relieved of their farm so needed to return to their town property. So Peter decided we should buy a house in this recession and take advantage of the cheaper prices. We had a great choice with so many people leaving and finally decided on a delightful two storey continental style house on Loresho Ridge which was set in six acres of grounds. There was also a 3 bedroomed cottage on the land, which we would be able to rent out. We were very pleased and content with our find. We were not to know that this place would be Peter's last home.

CHAPTER TWENTY

BUSY DAYS IN THE MINISTRY

I had never realised how very exhausting people can be until I became a Minister's Secretary. I was thrown into what seemed a sea of faces with thousands of voices that pleaded, flattered, threatened, wheedled and bewildered me. The telephones on my desk fought with each other to ring the greatest number of times, and the voices from these competed with the crowds of people who inundated my office from early morning until I escaped hopefully by 6pm. Something had to be done! I gradually sorted out who and what was important and achieved some semblance of order, but it was impossible to cut down to a peaceful level. After two weeks Lawrence Sagini grinned at me and said,

"You're doing fine!"

Somehow I managed to cope and later enjoyed the hectic pace.

The Assistant Minister and the Permanent Secretary were Africans, the Under Secretary was an Asian lady and all the Officers of the Ministry were still Europeans. We were a happy, compatible team. Early mornings would be spent liaising with them, in order of priority, as to who could spend time with the Minister that day for discussions on Ministry business. Keeping the duplicate diaries of the Minister and myself was a nightmare task for appointments often had to be made for weeks and months ahead. At 9.30am the Minister would arrive and commence sorting out the enormous pile of secret and confidential papers, top priority letters and other documents which I had placed on his desk. I would then lock the outer doors and attach 'Do not Disturb' notices so that he could swiftly and competently dictate replies to this awesome mound of paper. At 11am we spent a coffee break during which he would explain many things that lightened my burden. Being a humorous person, he had a wonderful knack of relaxing the tensions created in this enormously responsible work area, thus keeping us all happy. As a family man with five children he loved to tell me all about them, and he was always very interested to hear about my family in return. After our little break he would resignedly ask,

"Now who have you got for me today?"

Perhaps there would be another Minister, two or three members of our own Ministry, perhaps a couple of important members of his constituency of Kisii, maybe a new Ambassador paying his respects, or visiting District Commissioners from up-country, sometimes the Mayor of Nairobi. As I ushered them through I would desperately try in between to type the correspondence he had just dictated as I might not see him again for signatures that day.

There were Cabinet Meetings, Parliamentary Questions in the House, official luncheons, cocktail parties, and dinners, official trips all over the country to Local Government Offices, functions such as the opening of new buildings, and overseas trips all to cope with and arrange. On many occasions I lunched with him in Parliament Buildings as this was the only time available for us to cope with the amount of work flowing in. I attended the first Official Opening of the new Kenya Parliament, and was suitably impressed when the Speaker of the House, the Hon. Humphrey Slade, kept a dignified and correct order throughout the proceedings. Jomo Kenyatta was arrayed in a magnificent leopard skin robe with hat to match. Sometimes I would sit in for a while at Parliamentary sessions if I had had to rush over with amendments to a question Mr. Sagini was answering that afternoon, when I would become enthralled in the business at hand.

Peter and I were invited to so many functions; cocktail parties, luncheons, dinners, garden parties at State House, etc. I had to accompany Mr. Sagini on several official trips to Mombasa, Nakuru, Nanyuki, the one to Mombasa being for four days, where we had a very full programme. We stayed in the Oceanic Hotel and gave an official luncheon there. I was suddenly aware, at that table, that I was the only white person and the only female! Peter flew down for the day to spend Sunday with us and I was allowed to wander off with him for the afternoon. He seemed much better and happy these days for which I was so thankful and relieved.

Sometime later I noticed that Lawrence Sagini did not look well and always seemed tired. Each weekend, whenever possible, his driver would take him from his home near Nairobi, to Kisii, where he had a dairy farm and tea estate. His wife Mary, and the children, spent most of their time there. He loved this break and I'm sure Monday morning came round far too quickly when he had to rush back to the office. But even up there he had to spend so much of his valuable time keeping his constituents happy, and held many Sunday meetings.

One Friday morning he asked for a glass of water. Ten minutes later he called for another one and a short time later wondered if we had a jug I could fill for him. I looked to see if he was feverish as it was a cold day. Not wishing to appear concerned, which might have upset him, I kept the supply of water going, but secretly knew there was something very wrong. That evening he drove to Kisii, but by Saturday night he was a very sick man and was rushed back to Nairobi Hospital, where diabetes was diagnosed. I knew nothing of this until Monday morning when he rang me from the hospital telling me to go there with all the papers. He was a marvellous man, not at all concerned about himself, but thoroughly engrossed in medical literature about diabetes. He exclaimed,

"Did not Our Lord design the human body as a fantastic and intricate machine? Just look at these diagrams! And isn't modern medicine absolutely wonderful!" he followed on.

He could not have felt well but went through all the work I had brought and then said,

"I'll soon be fine, but I have to stay in here for ten days so the doctors can fix up my balanced treatment so, Louise, you must make this the office."

I tried to keep work to a minimum level and bothered him as little as possible. On a Monday morning I found him very agitated. He met me to say,

"Goodness, I forgot to send Jomo Kenyatta a cheque last week for his self-help hospital fund. You must go to State House immediately and hand it over to his Private Secretary."

Jomo Kenyatta's slogan of 'Harambee!' meaning 'work together' or 'pull together', had resulted in many projects going ahead such as the building of hospitals, schools and clinics in country areas where Africans were expected to work and give to build up their country and his Ministers were definitely expected to set a good example.

"You must go at once and please apologise for me and say I forgot with being sick."

I felt somewhat uncomfortable seeing him act so guiltily but I agreed to take the cheque. He rang State House to give them my car number so that I could pass the sentries at the gates. As I drove to State House I wondered how I had allowed myself to get into this position. We could have had the cheque delivered by internal mail, but obviously he was very worried by the delay. I felt embarrassed as the sentries waved me through the imposing gates. At the main entrance to the house I was met by a police officer who led me through the great hall of Government House and down several passages, finally knocking on a door where I was admitted into the Private Secretary's office. I had been pleased to note on the way that everything was still beautifully maintained in Britain's last bastion. I handed over the envelope to a friendly gentleman who chatted with me pleasantly and was just on the point of leaving when a side door was flung open and there was Kenya's leader.

"What's this? What's this then?" he queried.

I was introduced and the reason for my visit explained. He shook hands with me, his eyes meanwhile searching my face intently. I felt uncomfortable for they were very strange eyes. He seemed pleased and told me to inform Mr. Sagini that he hoped he would soon feel better and that everything was alright; he was not to worry. As I turned to leave he flicked his fly whisk which caught me playfully in the rear. I did not look round and walked away down the passage when he shouted behind me,

"Good-bye and thank you".

This helped to dissolve any indignation I might have been feeling; I still fostered many mixed feelings about the man who had been leader of the Kenya African Union. I remembered all the atrocities and bloodshed of both black and white human beings, predominantly black. Time was to prove him an overpowering leader of a one party state who put down any unrest swiftly and expediently, thus maintaining Kenya as a good example of a peaceful independent African nation which was to remain so until the time of his death and after.

When Lawrence Sagini returned to work, a trip to Garissa was organised. This was an adventure for me as we were visiting the northern desert area of Kenya where the inhabitants were chiefly Somalis. We flew there in a 9 seater Police Air Wing plane piloted by a veteran, Punch Bearcroft. He kept up a lively and humorous conversation with us as he steered us round tricky cloud formations, dodged the odd storm and deposited us safe and sound on the small airstrip where an Army Guard of Honour was waiting for the Minister.

The Army was there in full force as this was the time when the "Shifta" terrorists were at odds with Kenya, and Garissa was an easy target for them. The town had been protected by a boma of thick prickly thorn fencing rather like the hedges round Masai villages. Soldiers were on guard everywhere; jeeps and armoured cars escorted us to the areas where the Minister was to perform his various duties. He opened a school which we all toured; the children proudly sang the Kenya National Anthem. We visited the Council Offices where he held a meeting with the officers, and then we were taken to the District Commissioner's home for lunch. The house was situated on the banks of the Tana River, a striking contrast from the glaring white sand on which the town was built, for here were shady trees and flowering shrubs. Cool shady verandahs and rooms sheltered us from the heat of noon. We had passed many houses, white, with flat roofs and I had noticed the paths and driveways around them neatly lined with whitewashed stones which gave them a neat, clean and shining appearance.

Lunch was an African meal of tasty chops, possibly goat, with lots of fresh vegetables and fruit salad for dessert. The Garissa Officers were all Africans and their wives were eager to please and obviously excited with this visit of a Nairobi Minister. Some Somali girl visitors were tall, slender and truly beautiful, most of them dressed in white dresses of lace and silk which gave the occasion a festive atmosphere.

The afternoon was taken up by a huge public gathering at which the Minister made a speech. This was followed by entertainment when dancing and singing provided a colourful display. The Minister and his party were then presented with beautiful gifts, but unfortunately mine disappeared on the homeward journey - a carved tray and some pretty beads!

After this enthralling ceremony we were informed that some nomad Somalis were camped just outside the town and had sent a message inviting the Minister to meet them; would he please go out and say 'hello'. There was, of course, the possibility of Shifta snipers taking advantage of such an undertaking, but with a strong escort of army vehicles we fulfilled their wish. Lawrence met them with obvious interest. Several families were seated around rough shelters; camels were tethered to thorn trees. The heat and the myriad of flies, together with a potent stench from the camels and goats was quite something to contend with, but they seemed completely oblivious of all these discomforts. The men chatted and joked with us, the women laughed and giggled, and excited children ran around clapping their hands. As we were about to leave one of the men asked Mr. Sagini if he would like a ride on a camel which rather shattered him! The District Commissioner saved him by saying,

"Well, perhaps not a ride as there isn't time, but how about sitting on that one over there so that we can take a picture sir?"

It was a huge camel lying placidly on the ground, busy chewing its cud! Sagini eyed it suspiciously, but agreed, so several shots were taken of him alone, and with others. Maybe the camel was getting sick of all this frivolity at his expense when the Minister shouted for me to join him. I had just got seated, when to my horror the camel broke his tethering ropes and swiftly started to rise. We were both flung several yards into the crowd which caused much hilarity. The under-secretary managed to use her camera and take advantage of this unexpected action. Back in Nairobi the resultant pictures were a source of great mirth for some time to come!

We rounded off the day by taking tea with the Officers at the Army camp near the air strip. Many of these officers had been trained at Sandhurst in England and seemed very happy to reminisce with me on their time and activities in that country. We were reluctant to leave this happy socialising, but Punch Bearcroft urged us away as the aircraft had to reach Nairobi before dark or he would be unable to land; so off we had to go. What a memorable day it was for me as I never had the opportunity to revisit Garissa.

As we walked away from the plane at Wilson Airport in Nairobi I saw a familiar looking figure sitting on the airport fence. He was gazing intently over our way and I suddenly realised it was Peter. I had not been expecting him so it was a lovely surprise, and I waved excitedly for him to come over. As he drew near my heart jumped with fear, for there was a look of utter and complete sadness in his eyes and bearing. There was no chance to remark on this as we all moved through the airport buildings and chatted prior to leaving. Lawrence talked to him for quite some time as they were good friends, and gradually we all broke away to go to our respective homes. In the car, Peter had changed to his usual bright, gentle, affectionate manner and the haunting look had gone so I felt reassured. Later I was aware that this was the first time he knew there was a possibility of him dying from his disease, when I discovered he had been to see his doctor during the afternoon.

CHAPTER TWENTY ONE

OUR GREAT LOSS

(I gran dolori sono muti)

Shortly after my return from Garissa, Peter asked if we could all arrange to take two weeks leave from our respective posts for a holiday at the coast. He said we were all overdue for a rest and that he wanted to take us, the staff and even the animals for a complete change. My heart ached as I thought of the frequent visits he had been making to the doctor during the preceding weeks, but never at any time could I get him to discuss his illness with me. He had been losing weight, but always said he was fine. I kept my fears to myself as I did not wish to upset the girls, but I think they had a premonition that this trip was very important to him and they co-operated in every way. Somehow things fell into place and we were able to get away.

The journey to Mombasa passed in the same happy way except for a surprise lunch at a new hotel which had opened since our last trip down the road. One of Kenya's oldest white hunters had retired, and had now opened this attractive place. Peter really enjoyed looking round as he had designed the electrical installation for the premises. In the early evening we arrived at the house on the beach which he had rented for us, where everything looked perfect as always.

During the first week he was happy and cheerful, seemingly full of energy as he visited local hotels, swam, walked the dogs along the beach in the early evenings, explored historical buildings and looked round a visiting English warship which had called in at Mombasa harbour. But the second week was a very different story. Suddenly he could not eat; the sight of food revolted him; he could not sleep and tossed and turned all night long. He visibly lost more weight and spent the days lying on the beach, dozing fitfully or reading a book, the dogs beside him. I was not allowed to console him as he always insisted that nothing was wrong except perhaps a tummy upset. If I tried to sit by him on the beach, he almost seemed distressed and suggested that we should go off on trips without him, but we never did. Although the girls were concerned, I don't think at that stage they realised just how ill he was.

On the day of departure, he insisted on driving us back home, and although all four of us could drive, he never let up. Early that morning he walked down the beach and stood looking out to sea in the sad and forlorn way I had noticed at the airport a few weeks earlier. I watched him from the balcony, then ran down to grab his arm and say,

"Oh Peter, what is it? Please, please promise me you will see the doctor immediately we get back." He patted my hand and said that he would and I must not worry so.

On the way home he seemed brighter, pointing out all the things of interest, and stopping at all our favourite places where he lingered and enjoyed the cheerful comradeship of friends and acquaintances. When we drove up to our garage, the car radiator blew up suddenly with a huge, hissing bang. It was a Studebaker car of which he was very fond, and we found ourselves laughing and saying that at least it had been determined to get us home before it flew apart. Maybe it was an omen for he never drove the car again.

Next morning, I was shocked into near hysteria, when quietly he said,

"Darling, I am going into hospital today. The doctor arranged it all before we went to the coast. He just wants me to have a good check-up and you are not to worry, I don't think it will be for long. You will be pleased to know I am going into the Aga Khan hospital, so Elaine will keep an eye on me I'm sure."

I cried, but then felt better, because at least he would be resting and having the very best of attention under the care of the foremost specialist in Kenya. I drove him there in my car and followed him up the steps, where he squared his shoulders and marched in resolutely, cheerfully greeting the sisters on duty. He was given a nice private room, and we went through the usual formalities of signing in at a hospital. The sisters then asked me to leave. I forced myself to smile and show no distress as I left, saying that I would be back for the early evening visiting hours. I knew that Elaine would be peeping in from time to time which was a great comfort.

I remember that day I felt no deep anxiety, and as I ran back up the steps in the early evening, I was determined to be cheerful by telling him of all the day's events and giving him the salaams of Sacunda and all the staff. I was so happy to find him peacefully sitting in a chair, smoking his pipe and reading a book. Later, the girls joined us and we, as always, enjoyed a family get together, making it as jolly as possible. At 7pm the specialist arrived, and from the door, discreetly beckoned for me to join him outside. I knew him well as he had taken care of me after my eye trouble. I was full of questions as he guided me to a small room and sat me down on a chair. He asked how my eye was these days, and if he could make a small examination to see if it had settled down, which I impatiently endured as I was only interested in Peter's welfare. Then very seriously, he proceeded to inform me that Peter was a very sick man and that he was not certain if he could save him. Even if he did, he said, he could not promise him more than eighteen months of life. He was very, very kind, but oh, so definite.

How did I feel at such a time? I only remember a great numbness, a great vacuum which seemed to last an eternity, from which I gradually emerged into a bleak, miserable and entirely different world. My poor Peter, always so full of life, a wonderful husband and father, clever, kind, so young and good looking, and so dearly loved by many people. How could he be taken from us, it couldn't be true, it wasn't fair. I gazed sadly at Dr. Harries and tried to pull myself together.

"Does he know?" I whispered.

"I have told him that he is very sick and that he must remain here for a week or two," he consoled. "He knows that he has arteriosclerosis and atheroma and that we must treat his very high blood pressure with much stronger drugs. This, of course, is the real worry, as the human body can only stand so much, but there is one thing in his favour, he has a very strong heart."

He gave me more time to recover, then led me back to Peter's room where everything appeared so normal that what I had just experienced seemed a ghastly nightmare that would, that must, vanish.

I must not be morbid, I firmly told myself. After all, the doctor had not said he would die here and now; he had promised possibly eighteen months of life and how I clung to that thought. I was able to act cheerfully and give no sign of anything wrong as we all kissed him good night, promising to be back tomorrow. I rang him later from home to wish him a second good night when we exchanged more endearments and even joked a little. The girls had asked me on the way home what the specialist had said and I was able to reassure them that their father was going on a course of drugs for two weeks which should help him a lot.

For the next two or three days my fears were stilled as nothing untoward happened, but then came the first shock when we heard he had fallen out of bed during the night. He was not found for some time, and he later told me that he must have blacked out for when he came round he wondered where on earth he was, as he was lying under the bed looking up at the bedsprings, which he did not recognise as such! However, once over that episode, he again progressed favourably. The first Sunday morning we called in to see him as we had been invited to a picnic lunch with a friend. He was pleased, and told us to enjoy ourselves and not hurry back as it was such a lovely day. Halfway through the picnic, why did I feel so restless, so apprehensive, so unbearably lonely. I jumped up and exclaimed,

"Come, we must get back!"

I knew as we re-entered the hospital that something dreadful had happened. We were told that he had suffered a stroke which had deprived him of speech. My heart broke as I gazed down at him lying there on the pillows. I took his hand, and his eyes told me that he could understand all I was saying, but the agony, to him, of not being able to reply was so apparent that I had to turn away. That day, I knew I must prepare the girls for what might happen. After the first shock, they refused to accept the blow, and like me, clung to the hope of eighteen months grace.

Our friends were a tremendous support in our great trouble. Lawrence Sagini refused to allow me to work until Peter showed signs of improvement, and he came to the hospital each day, as did our friend, Father Grogan. I stayed at the hospital night and day for five weeks, each day of which the doctors expected him to die. Sad to say, our loved one gradually slipped away as his kidneys finally stopped working. His great will to live made him fight tenaciously, but fate denied him the wish and deprived us of ever hearing him speak again, or ever taking him home. The night he died, I had lived and re-lived the moment so often, I felt nothing except a dumb and final acceptance with no tears. Earlier in the evening, I had walked in the hospital gardens with Father Grogan, a man who had sat with me until midnight each night and who had re-appeared for a quick call each morning at 8.30 to give me strength and courage, a man so worthy of the name priest, who I will never forget. I think he knew that this would be the night and did not leave at the midnight hour; he was with us when Peter left us at 3am.

Gradually I collected myself and hugged my sobbing daughters. Father Grogan now took us under his wing, driving us home, preparing hot tea and sedatives for us all. He then disappeared, returning some time later from the direction of the bedrooms to say,

"Come now, you must rest. I thought it would be more comforting for you all to sleep in one room so I have made up some beds for you all in the main room. Do try to sleep a little now as there will be so much to see to in the next twelve hours. I will return at 8am."

The shock had turned us into clockwork toys, quietly doing as we were told. It was already 4.30am but I think we all slept a little at some stage, from sheer exhaustion. We clung to each other, spending most of the time in my large bed.

Sacunda roused us at 7am with morning tea. From his face, wrinkled with grief, I knew that he already had the news. He said Father Grogan had aroused him at 4.30am telling him to take care of us. He was magnificent, saying all the right things, helping us to get moving, running baths, ordering the cook to prepare a light breakfast which he urged us to eat. As we sat at the table, Lawrence and Mary Sagini arrived.

Lawrence had rung the hospital at 7am and on hearing the news had immediately dashed over with his wife to see what they could do. He was very upset, as he was due to fly off at 10am to speak at a large meeting in western Kenya, from which he could not be excused.

Unhappily he fretted that he could not spend this day with us and attend the funeral. Later, as he and his wife left, he pressed a small book into my hand, saying,

"Keep this little book and read a page each day. I know it will help you. Someone gave it to me when my mother died. I was far away, studying in America at the time and it saved me from unbearable sorrow."

I glanced at the title, "The Bread of Life", which meant nothing to me then, but how that book comforted me in the months ahead.

Father Grogan arrived; friends commenced phoning, others came to the house. In a daze, we helped with the necessary arrangements for a funeral at 4pm that day; death certificates, cemetery plot, coffin, newspaper and radio adverts, pall bearers, hymns for the funeral service, flowers, veils and the catering for the people who would be returning to the house after the funeral. Perhaps it was good to be so active, but it was a bad dream, it couldn't be happening to us, I told myself. I was still numb with shock, no tears, no real feelings. The girls were wonderful, giving their all to these necessary affairs.

We stood in the beautiful cathedral at 4pm, where it seemed even more dreamlike, listening to the words of the burial service. Some of Peter's best friends were pall bearers. How sad they looked, how gently they handled his last resting place. Then came the convoy to the cemetery. Before the graveside ceremony I was cheered to see so many, many friends, business associates, Officers of the Ministry and others, giving their support and paying their last respects to our beloved Peter, most of them visibly moved. Sacunda and John standing there, deeply grieved by the loss of their bwana. I felt so proud of him. What a wonderful and respected person he had been. As the coffin gently descended into the grave I felt his arms around me, dragging me down, down with him for ever. I swayed, then rocked backwards and the sensation had gone.

My family saved me in the days that followed; my thoughts were all of them. How I cherished their presence, their loving care and attention. I helped them too through the difficult times when I knew they missed their father the most. Father Grogan was a saint, endowed with inexhaustible patience and devotion, who came to visit us each evening, staying until midnight or even 1am, I knew, intentionally to tire us out, so that we would fall asleep from sheer exhaustion once we retired to our beds. When the therapy worked, he gradually cut down his visits to three nights per week, then two, then just weekly. He knew exactly when to change the pattern and was also aware of the time when we began to take notice of things and start to live again.

Three days after the funeral, Lawrence Sagini rang me to say that I should return to work. He said it was bad for me to stay alone and that he and all the staff at the Ministry wished to have me there so they could cheer and comfort me. I agreed, and the girls also resumed their duties. We kept busy, busy all the time, but for quite a long period when we drove up to our home in the evenings, we could not bear to go inside; home without Peter upset us so much. We would turn round at the gate and go for another ride so that when we returned, Father Grogan would be there. Sacunda suffered with us. He tried in every way to keep our home cheerful and bright, even gathering and arranging flowers in all the rooms and organising delicacies to whet our appetites. He joked with us, but his heart was sad.

Only time can heal the deep sadness, but never, never ease the loneliness of losing such a loved one.

CHAPTER TWENTY TWO

PICKING UP THE PIECES

Before his death, Peter had commenced negotiations to buy the house at Loresho Ridge. The agent now enquired if I wished to carry on with the purchase. We all realised that we still needed a home, and could not bring ourselves to leave Kenya at this stage, despite pleas from grandparents and friends in England to come home. To us, Kenya was home, and although Peter was no longer with us, we felt his spirit all around, so I agreed to go ahead. The owner of the property was living in Australia, and the agent explained it would take a few weeks to finalise the deal and that he would keep in touch.

This gave us a new interest in the place, which was good, and we were kept occupied at weekends painting the cottage which we wished to rent out. We also agreed to have a doctor's son, who was studying engineering in Nairobi, come and stay with us during the week. His parents resided in Kericho where he returned at weekends. It was wise to have a male around the house whilst armed robbery was still a regular occurrence in the suburbs, and Robert was a cheerful, kind boy who was very good company. The painting accomplished, we rented the cottage to a young married couple.

We were all, of course, very much occupied during the week in our various careers. I had been excused from attending too many social events as Lawrence Sagini realised that I was unhappy and not yet ready to mingle with other happy couples at these affairs; I was much more at ease just visiting my own very close friends. And so, gradually, we were picking up the pieces, surviving, clinging to each other, our friends and the familiar surroundings of our beloved Kenya.

Unfortunately, this bearable lifestyle was about to be cruelly shattered. One Sunday we received a visit from a family who informed us that they were the new owners of the property and that they would like to look round. They also said they would be taking possession at the end of the month. I smiled as I told them they must be at the wrong house, that this one belonged to us, or would be ours very shortly. The man laughed back, unfeelingly, almost gloatingly as he replied,

"Oh no! I'm afraid not. You see we beat you to it. We went over your agent's head and made a direct cash offer to the owner in Australia. She has accepted it and we have paid her direct from London."

He went on, "We need to move in urgently, so I'm sorry but we cannot give you more than a month."

We were completely stunned. I rang the agent who was just as flabbergasted, for he knew nothing of the deal. He wired the owner who confirmed that it was sold, which filled him with dismay at our plight. How uprooted, insecure and miserable our situation now seemed.

The event that followed a few days later unsettled us to such a degree that for the first time we thought it might be best for us to even leave Kenya. As Sacunda entered with the morning tea, I knew immediately that something dreadful had happened. He dare not speak, but just waved for me to follow him. What a shambles met my eyes as I entered the living quarters of the house. Almost everything except heavy furniture had been taken from every room, or the remainder left in chaos on the floors. The kitchen and stores had also been raided, leaving us without crockery, pots and pans and other necessary utensils. The week's wash was missing from the laundry, plus all the shoes left there for cleaning. Robert's golf clubs and tennis rackets were also gone from the hall cupboard.

"Oh dear Lord!" I thought, "What next?"

We had not heard a sound in the night. The bedrooms were locked off down a long corridor, so luckily for us they had left that part of the house, perhaps deciding they had collected sufficient loot for one night. The most frightening thing was to find they had gained entry by cutting a large hole in the solid wood of the sturdy back door which was also protected by padlocked iron bars inside. We had thought the house completely burglar proof with these precautions at each door and wrought iron screens over each window, which proved us so wrong when they were prepared to go to such lengths to gain entry. Our guardian, Robert, was completely shattered. We discussed why we had not been able to hear them, why, at least, had the dogs not barked, why had the servants not heard them.

It was a complete mystery, especially when we found the tracks of a large vehicle in the driveway. The morning was spent with the police and insurance people, but of course, we knew we would never see our possessions again. The remainder of our time in the house was very unhappy with the new owners pestering us at all hours, a tedious invasion of our privacy. Not content with robbing our home from under our feet we had to suffer this further indignity. Quietly, and very thoughtfully, I began to make plans for our future.

Although our lives, post independence and prior to Peter's death, had not been too hassled, we knew that many frightening events had been taking place in other peoples' lives. White girls went through a trying time when some of the newly formed society of educated Africans placed in well paid posts decided that a Mercedes car and a white girl friend were desired status symbols. There was sex harassment in offices with threats to these girls of being deported if they did not comply.

Deportation at short notice of twenty four hours was a threat over all whites. It could be for as little as using an old street name instead of the new African names which the streets had received. It was difficult not to do this sometimes when one had used the old ones for many years. Any criticism of Jomo Kenyatta or any political figure aired in offices or restaurants, if overheard by an informer, also meant a swift exit. The Europeans joked and cautioned each other,

"Watch it or you will be on the midnight plane!" But it was not a laughing matter as these people's assets were confiscated.

Africans also would enter Indian shops and order clothing, shoes, furniture, TV's, cars, foodstuffs, alcohol etc. They did not pay. The despairing Indians would send out the statements month after month with no result. They were too afraid to sue and suffered great losses. However, in later years Jomo Kenyatta intervened and they had to pay. Corruption had led to Africans obtaining driving licences without passing tests. Thus the toll of road accidents was appalling. We all had to develop a sixth sense when driving. Africans would tell a European to go to the bank and get them money. They truly believed that a white person could do this ad lib and that it did not have to be deposited there first before he could.

We also suffered from missing mail. We waited anxiously for letters from overseas people and wondered if they received ours. The mail sorters were now Africans who apparently got rid of letters to save sorting or if they had handwriting they could not understand. Eventually, there was a massive blockage in the sewer pipes of Nairobi Post Office. European inspectors found all our missing mail! Corruption payments became necessary to receive tax clearance, licences, permits for businesses etc. Wild animals were being slaughtered by poachers for ivory.

I spoke to Lawrence Sagini, saying I was thinking of taking the girls to South Africa and then on to England to see if they would care to spend their future days in either of these places; it was a choice they should have now that Peter was gone. He was, as always, wonderful; he knew that conditions for white people in Kenya were not particularly stable, but emphasised that he would never wish us to leave. Perhaps it would be good to do this trip, he advised; get everything into perspective and have a complete rest and change from all the sorrow and anxieties of the past months. Then, the old smile and twinkling eyes as he said,

"You'll be back. Oh yes! You'll come back."

Robert and the nice young tenants departed. Some of the furniture was stored, the remainder sold. The girls gave in their notices at work and I resigned from the Ministry. The day of my farewell to Local Government was a memorable and moving occasion, with a ceremony that took me completely by surprise. At 10am a reporter and a cameraman from the Ministry of Information arrived at the office. I had no entry in the diary so joked with them that they had the wrong day or the wrong office. They replied,

"No, the Minister is expecting us."

Sagini now flung open his office door, beckoning them to enter as he smiled at me and said,

"It's alright."

There was complete silence for quite some time behind the closed door, then suddenly the under-secretary emerged asking me to please come in. I was bewildered, what on earth was going on, how had she got in there without my knowledge! To my astonishment I found the room full of people, members of the Ministry and others. The conference table was laden with drinks, snacks, glasses and plates. In the background the camera was at the ready; Lawrence came forward to take my hand as it commenced to roll. He made a beautiful parting speech, ending with the presentation of flowers and lovely gifts from himself and all present. I was overwhelmed, and tears were very close, as I verbally tried to acknowledge their good wishes, feeling altogether humbled and honoured by this concessive display of their affection.

I shall always remember Lawrence Sagini as a man with a heart of gold. Secretly, he had arranged this touching farewell party, quietly gathering in the participants through his outside office door, plus all the food and drinks. Later, he told me that when he missed the reporter and the cameraman, he was afraid that I might have guessed what was in store and that I might have become nervous.

At home, that evening, I was startled to hear the headline on the Kenya news,

"Minister says farewell to his Personal Secretary."

I gazed at the TV screen, reliving the ceremony and eyeing myself critically. I wished I could have had time, at least, to comb my hair before I was called in! My daughter, Maureen at the TV station had excitedly edited the film when she found it was of her Mum. She later presented me with a copy, which I treasure.

We spent a hectic time sorting out an itinerary for our journeying, and agreed that we should go to South Africa first by boat, which would give us the time for a relaxing holiday. Then, if South Africa did not please us, we would return and fly on to England later.

Departure day was drawing near, and the most dreaded partings still to come: Sacunda, John and Andrea. They knew we were going, of course. The greater tolerance of youth to change in life was apparent in John and Andrea who were quickly fixed up with new posts, but still they were very sorry we were leaving. Sacunda's bearing told a different story. He was now in his eighties. How could we console him. I gently argued that he was long overdue for retirement, overdue to spend some time resting and enjoying his last years on beautiful Kilimanjaro, in the company of his friends and relatives. He looked at me with stony eyes,

"Hii kazi buri, memsahib!"

I smiled reminiscently. He had given me the same answer the first day he came to work for us, years ago, when I had asked him if he had a wife and family. As near as possible in translation, it had meant then, 'No. That is spare work!' Now in this case, 'It is of little consequence in life.'

I knew he was clinging to the hope that we would return, that we would not settle away from Kenya, that we would come back.

"Mimi ngoja, memsahib, mimi ngoja." (I will wait, memsahib, I will wait.)

"I will miss you, and remember you always," was my lame, inadequate reply.

And so, we insecure, unhappy and undecided females prepared to depart for 'Foreign Lands' to search for a future we hoped would be happier, settled and more suitable to our needs.

CHAPTER TWENTY THREE

SOUTH AFRICA

At the last moment, Maureen was prevented from accompanying us on our travels to South Africa and England, as Kenya Television were not happy about breaking the contract she had with them, especially as they found it very difficult to replace qualified staff. She did not appear to mind too much, and said she was happy for us to make a judgement on those two countries, where she could join us once we had made a decision. I suspected a boy friend in the background was responsible for her placid acceptance of the situation! Nevertheless, we were very sorry not to have her with us, and anxious for her welfare. Happily, Sacunda was saved; he was able to stay on and take care of her in a small cottage she rented. Our staunch friends promised to care for her too.

Val, Elaine and I proceeded by train to Mombasa, where we boarded the Rhodesia Castle for a round trip to Durban. This was the Rhodesia Castle's last voyage, after which she would return to England to be scrapped, but we found no fault with her capabilities on this journey. We sailed on the morning tide, just at dawn, when the throbbing of the engines awoke us from a deep sleep. We dashed on deck in time to espy our little white house at Likoni, reminding us of the many times we had sat there gazing at ships such as this one, not so very long ago.

As we reached the open sea, the passengers and ship's officers seemed to change into holiday mood almost immediately, which set the atmosphere for the whole trip and we always remember it as a happy time. The organised activities were not pressurised, the officers always helpful and courteous, and the food was magnificent. It was good for me to see Val and Elaine so relaxed and obviously enjoying themselves.

Our first port of call was Dar-es-Salaam in Tanzania, where we stopped over for two days. The harbour is quite beautiful, and is known as the harbour of peace, but the climate not so good as it is very hot and humid. The first day, being Sunday, we decided to visit the cathedral on the waterfront for the morning service. It was packed with people, and with very little air getting into the building, coupled with the odour from several hundreds of perspiring bodies, we found lasting out the whole service quite an ordeal and hoped that God would forgive us for being so restless.

The following day we joined a coach tour round the city where important buildings were pointed out to us; a large hotel and a museum completed the sight-seeing. We were not too impressed, comparing it with our own Nairobi, but the following drive round a bay, where Government House and the suburban housing were situated, was very pleasant. We then drove out of town a few miles to see old Arab trading posts, and some small mosques, which were much more interesting. We also visited an African village where the natives had quite large corks embedded in their upper lips. They looked grotesque, but seemed unaffected by this marring of their features, as they happily escorted us round their huts and a market place, where, of course, they hoped we would make a few purchases.

Next day we sailed on for Beira in, then, Portuguese Mozambique. This was the time when an oil embargo had been placed on Rhodesia after she declared unilateral independence from Great Britain. Beira was the port used by Rhodesia, so British naval vessels were patrolling the Indian Ocean in this area, in order to enforce the embargo. We saw several of these ships carrying out their lonely vigil, and passed quite close to one or two, whose crews waved and cheered us on our way. Our ship returned the greetings by hooting merrily in reply. We stayed in Beira for only a few hours, just long enough for a walk into town where we visited a restaurant for a cool drink. The shops had very little in stock to attract one; the city was quite dead and dirty so we did not linger. Because of the tensions of the Rhodesian situation, the docks were guarded by a large contingent of Portuguese soldiers, who appeared to be quite bored and restless. It was not a happy place so we were not sorry to move on.

Our next call we enjoyed immensely. This was at Lorenzo Marques, also in Mozambique, a real show place after Beira. The city had a clean and sparkling appearance with its magnificent white marble buildings, statues and churches. The wide, tree-lined streets and mosaic footpaths, a splendid luxury hotel, and a Catholic cathedral architecturally similar to the one we had visited in Masaka, Uganda, but on a much grander scale, were all features that made it an exciting and, to us, unusual place. The local inhabitants were friendly and helpful, so altogether we enjoyed a wonderful three day visit.

On one of our tourist coach trips, we were a little subdued to hear that our first call would be at a cemetery. However, we found it an overwhelmingly moving experience, not in a sad way, but rather like a visit to an eternal city. The cemetery covered a very large acreage, and one gazed at seemingly endless rows of marble headstones which were quite fantastic in design with large carved angels and statues. Several had photographs of the deceased embedded in the headstones. There were many family tombs where there would be a small room which had curtained door and windows. There would be a table and chairs in the room with flowers and photographs on the table. The coffins lay on marble shelves at each side. We saw several family members seated in some of these who appeared happy and peaceful. I gathered they were speaking to their departed loved ones, obviously without sorrow, but rather with a great deal of comfort.

I remember the pigeons at Lorenzo Marques fluttering down in their hundreds to courtyards and streets, unafraid and inquisitive. Glancing through an archway one afternoon I saw a flock landing in a picturesque old courtyard where many of them perched on the edge of a well.

"Oh Peter! Isn't that beautiful?" I involuntarily gasped.

My Peter was not there in the flesh, but somehow that day I knew he was very near in spirit and happy to see us enjoying this trip. I felt his presence very strongly as we journeyed along.

Nearing Durban, we awoke one day to find the ship swaying uncomfortably from side to side. Moving around was quite unpleasant, but we managed to gather in the dining room where it was quite upsetting to see blue sky through the portholes one moment, and grey sea the next! Still unaffected, the girls and I commenced eating. It was not long before other passengers disappeared one by one and then it was my turn. I had a long dash up two flights of stairs and down a long corridor. Banging open my bathroom door I almost fell over the steward who was busy washing the floor. He quickly escaped, returning shortly with a glass of something he asked me to drink. I protested that I couldn't face it, but he insisted, for which I was truly grateful, as I immediately felt better. I never knew what it was, but it certainly put me right. Luckily, the girls were not affected, but most of the other passengers did not appear again that day. We were told there had been a tidal wave which had hit Durban and that the ship was feeling the after flow. She continued with her swaying dance until we thankfully berthed in the South African city.

Our stay in Durban was for four or five days, but most of the passengers were still feeling queasy, and the ship's doctor was busily occupied handing out bottles of medicine for nervous stomachs. Feeling fine, the girls and I set out to explore the city. We found a long line of taxis near the ship and were surprised to see that the drivers of these were large boned, muscular ladies wearing mens'' tweed caps! They looked capable and tough, similar to some of the men taxi drivers we were to meet later in Rome. We avoided them, and made our way along the sea front where we were concerned to see the damage caused by the tidal wave. Amusement park buildings had been smashed and swept back from the foreshore. The road was badly damaged, and underground piping exposed and lifted for great distances. It all looked desolate, but not knowing how the area looked normally, we were unable to estimate the full impact of this occurrence.

We saw young Zulus with their rickshaws, eager to take us on a trip to town. They were of fine physique, and colourfully arrayed with large head-dresses, a splendid sight as they took off with their customers at great pace. We had to decline the inviting experience as suddenly we all felt ill. Perhaps it was the reaction of feeling solid ground under our feet after the turbulent period on the boat. We decided to find a seat where we could sit by the sea and recover. We now experienced the first sign of apartheid as the seats we found were marked, 'Whites only', 'Blacks only', etc., which was rather frustrating as we had to walk quite a long way before we found one we could use. As the area was quite deserted, it seemed unnecessary to us, and a disturbing, new experience. Our first day being spoiled, we returned to the ship to rest.

Next day was much better as we toured the city and department stores where the wonderful display of goods for sale, at very low prices, enticed us to go on a shopping spree. We visited parks and the botanical gardens, saw the suburban housing, also the markets. From the brow of a hill we looked down on an African housing area, which we were proudly informed had its own housing, schools, churches and a hospital. Later, in the main post office in town we discovered separate queues of 'Whites' and 'Blacks', for the purchase of stamps, an unfamiliar arrangement to us as never had there been any distinction of this nature in Kenya.

The climate was rather sultry in the month of May, and a thick haze hung over the city, making it difficult to take good photographs. Although Durban was a pleasant place, we did not somehow feel attracted by it, and had planned to spend the remaining time on out of city tours so that we could assess the surrounding countryside. Unfortunately, we were informed that night that the ship was leaving earlier than anticipated, so our stay was abruptly curtailed. Although very disappointed, I doubt on looking back, if a longer stay would have induced us to make South Africa our home. Maybe we were not ready for change, or perhaps the apartheid laws gave us an unpleasant discomfort, but we really felt no regret at being snatched away, just a little cheated, as our boat sailed away.

A number of Rhodesians had now boarded the Rhodesia Castle to travel to Beira, many of them returning from holiday-making. At the Sunday morning service, many passengers, including quite a few of these Rhodesians, gathered in the Common Room. The captain commenced the service by playing a recording of "God Save the Queen", whereupon all the Rhodesians walked out! This left behind a strained, uncomfortable atmosphere in the room which the captain broke up by asking for a volunteer to play the piano, in order to accompany the hymn singing. There was no response for some time, until an elderly lady pushed her husband forward. He seemed a little hard of hearing as the captain instructed him on which hymns to play. There followed a very amusing incident as we were asked to sing verses one to five of a certain hymn. At the end of the five verses the old gentleman carried on playing.

The captain tapped him on the shoulder, to no avail, as he valiantly played on, one verse, two verses, three verses. The embarrassed captain now walked round the piano player gesturing for him to stop but no, he just carried on. His wife shouted, but obviously he could not hear her. The perplexed captain now gave him a push, which practically unseated him, but at least he stopped! The ship's officers were lined up at the side of the dais, holding their caps in front of them, and when this occurred, many of them had to place the caps in front of their faces to hide their amusement. As the captain sternly swung round, they swiftly sprang to attention as they saw he was upset and obviously feeling a bit of a fool. These odd little moments of humour in life stick in the mind!

We chatted with several of the Rhodesians on the way to Beira. They felt betrayed by Britain's actions and said they would never give up fighting for their rights.

"Oh Africa!" I thought. "What will happen to this lovely continent in the years that lie ahead? Certainly great unrest, certainly bloodshed and economic disaster, with the real sufferers being the working people of all races. What a mixed up world!"

At Beira we were held up for three days and became very bored with the inactivity. The Rhodesians all left to either drive or go by rail to their respective homes up-country. The Portuguese soldiers on the docks appeared even more morose and lethargic. We had hoped for a further call at Lorenzo Marques, but this had been cut out of the itinerary and we would, instead, be calling at Dar-es-Salaam and the island of Zanzibar.

We seemed destined to spend Sundays in Dar-es-Salaam, but this time we missed church and lazily spent the time along the waterfront. Here there were large, shady trees and plenty of seating, so we were able to observe the local population going their various ways, also the movement of ships and small yachts in and out of this perfect harbour.

The weather was beautiful, the water calm and still, on the afternoon we left. Smoothly, the ship sailed out to sea. Looking back from our comfortable chairs on deck, as we listened to soft music filtering through the loud-speakers, we watched the town and Government House slowly fade from view. Later, a wonderful sunset brought a feeling of great peace and tranquillity, another unforgotten moment of our trip.

Unfortunately, we did not arrive off Zanzibar until after dark, but a full moon lit up the island and flickered over the sea. Silhouettes of palms sheltering white Arab buildings gave an artistic effect. A strong scent of cloves wafted through the air, bearing out Zanzibar's other name, the island of cloves. We were to be greatly disappointed, as after anchoring off shore, a Government launch brought officers to our ship who gave orders that no American or British passengers would be allowed ashore. As all passengers were of these nationalities, we were rather stunned. However, we should probably have anticipated something of this nature, as not very long before our trip, news had reached Nairobi that Julius Nyerere of Tanzania had been reported missing for some days. Also that the Kenyan and Tanzanian armies were in a state of mutiny, and large convoys of military vehicles, manned by unknown forces, were proceeding through the back country of Kenya towards Uganda. Fortunately, these vehicles were captured, the mutinies quelled and Julius Nyerere was back in office in Dar-es-Salaam. Strange to say, from that time onwards, he always wore the Chinese communist tunic. A later statement informed us that the island of Zanzibar had been taken over by forces of a communist element. It was one of those mysterious, never explained, historical events. Very soon Chinese workers arrived in Tanzania and built a railroad.

Having accepted the rebuff from the new authorities, we decided to settle down for the night, when over the loudspeakers came the news that persons of any nationality would be allowed ashore! Not trusting the new directive, there were no takers, as we all ignored the invitation. Again, trying to settle for the night, we became aware of an armada of small craft surrounding our ship. Swarms of Arabic and Arab mixture natives were now screaming for permission to come aboard with their wares. Soon, the decks were transformed into a market place, and despite our resentment, we could not resist purchasing such items as real amber jewellery, genuine ivory carvings and fans, Zanzibar chests, jewel boxes decorated with brass and ivory and many other treasures. These we bought at ridiculously low prices with no bargaining. In fact, the dealers seemed desperate to sell them at any price, which caused us to wonder just how bad things were under the new regime.

Next day we reached Mombasa and soon, Nairobi, where we were reunited with Maureen and our friends. Still, we did not linger, for having decided that South Africa was not the answer, we commenced preparations for our visit to Rome and England. The urge to keep travelling was with us. I have always found that at the end of any journeying, it is very difficult to settle down, and if I were a very rich person I am sure that I would still be wandering round the face of the earth.

CHAPTER TWENTY FOUR

ENGLAND

We felt almost guilty leaving Maureen working hard in Nairobi, as once again we flew off with British Airways for Rome, where we would stay for one week. At the Travel Agents we had been informed that we could break the journey at Rome and spend a very reasonable holiday there if we stayed at a certain address they gave us. This was supposedly a place run by nuns in order to make money for charitable purposes, so we had agreed to partake of this offer, both for our pocket's sake and for any help we might be giving to needy people.

Soon we were flying over Rome and could distinctly pick out the seven hills and St. Peter's Dome from the air. A taxi whizzed us along the road from the airport. It was early evening in the month of June; the scenery a subdued beige and gold followed by a haze of brown buildings in the eternal city. The taxi made its way through several thoroughfares, passing the Colosseum and other historical buildings which were easily recognisable. We kept an awed silence as their impact conjured up visions of days of yore.

Finally we turned into a narrow alley, jerked to a halt outside a building we mistook for a warehouse, and were told by the driver that this was it! Puzzled, we alighted, collected our luggage and found the taxi gone in a flash. Looking up and down the street we found that all the buildings were uniform with just a large double door and no windows at ground level, only a few shuttered ones very high up near the roofs. Could we be at the right address! I noticed a handle in the wall near the door and pulled it. In the distance a bell could be heard clanging loudly, but nothing happened. I tried again; no response. The third time we heard a grumbling female voice followed by the opening of the door. She was obviously an overworked domestic, not pleased to see us, and even less so as we asked her in English if this was the right address. She gabbled something in Italian so progress was slow as we tried to make her understand. Impatiently she finally slammed the door on us. What a predicament - no taxi, mounds of luggage, and lost! A few curious bystanders had now gathered who tried to help but the language barrier defeated us. Luckily a priest came along the road who kindly asked in English if he could be of assistance. He was able to assure us that this was the correct address. He rang the bell once more, when to our surprise, it was answered by a pleasant looking lady who confirmed that she was expecting us. Feeling cheered we gladly followed her inside.

We were ushered into an ancient baggage lift which clanged us up to a landing outside a beautiful carved wooden door, through which we entered a large hall. Where were the nuns we thought as we gazed around? The lady took us into a room, with three beds and the usual facilities, then beckoned us to a large dining room where twelve people were seated round a table, clearly half-way through their evening meal. We had discovered by now that our lady knew very little English; the folk at the table greeted us in Italian and carried on their conversations in that language, followed by a stony silence when we could not reply. How we wished we had swotted a little Italian before making this trip. We were curious about our whereabouts as there was still no sign of any ecclesiastical staff, and it seemed to us only some ordinary kind of boarding house. We were given dishes of minestrone soup followed by large pieces of steak and green beans. As we finished, we quietly passed a few humorous remarks regarding our fellow diners as they seemed a rather odd crowd. Imagine our consternation when one young man, giving us a disapproving look, inquired in perfect English,

"How long are you staying in Rome?"

Very embarrassed, we now talked to him, asking how we could get around the places of interest, but he was not particularly helpful. We did gather that we were not situated in an easy area for transport.

Everyone disappeared at this stage so we retired to our room. It was uncomfortably hot; the windows closed and heavily shuttered. The mattresses were very lumpy, not at all conducive to a good night's sleep. At 3am we were all wide awake. Val and Elaine had been savagely bitten by what could only be bed bugs. I tried to open the windows but they could not have been opened for years and would not budge; we thought we would suffocate. Miserably, we endured the rest of the night with the certainty in mind that we would look round for other accommodation in the morning. However, from 7am onwards we looked in vain for the lady of the house. Not a soul was to be seen. Then at 9am the lady, not so pleasant to behold now, in a dirty dressing gown with curlers in her hair, appeared in the corridor. She was not at all anxious to serve us with breakfast, but we insisted and received a piece of dry bread and a muddy cup of coffee. We were glad to make our escape from this unusual and disappointing accommodation, at a cost much higher than promised by the Travel Agents in Nairobi, and we vowed never to be taken in again by this kind of "rip off" offer.

After a few enquiries at the air terminal we were directed to a small family hotel in a more central area. On arriving there we had our first encounter with a truculent taxi driver who tried to charge us an exorbitant fare. I objected, whereupon he pushed me across the street quite savagely. I was breathless at this unexpected attack, and most relieved to see a young man dashing out of the hotel who grabbed the luggage and told me not to worry as he would settle the taxi bill. He was one of the sons of the family who ran the hotel and luckily had witnessed our plight from a window. What a comfort it was for us to now find ourselves in a clean, attractive, happy atmosphere. We were given a lovely room which had a balcony from where we could look out over a pleasant treed square. We spent a happy time in this homely hotel; the family was delightful, the food excellent, the service without fault and the cost reasonable indeed!

We discovered that if we wished to go sightseeing, a coach called at the hotel each morning which would take us on various tours. We found this an unbelievable experience; in great comfort we were able to go out for five hours each day with couriers and interpreters for £1 each. We considered ourselves extremely lucky.

How very impressed and enthralled we were by these journeys into the past; the Colosseum, the Forum, the Trevi Fountains, the Spanish Steps, the Catacombs, the Appian Way, the Villa Borghese, Mussolini's Stadium, Castel Sant'Angelo, the Pantheon, a ride out to Tivoli where we toured the 4th century Villa D'Este with its fantastic, uncanny terraced garden fountains; all the old churches, St. Mary's, St. Mark's, St. John's, and the crowning glory of St. Peter's where we attended mass in one of the small chapels. One whole day was spent exploring the Vatican Museums where we walked miles without even noticing, so deeply absorbed we were in the treasures displayed there, including the great masters' paintings and the sublime Sistine Chapel. Our courier teased us on this day saying that if we were very good the Pope would speak to us! Sure enough, as we were herded to a certain position in St. Peter's Square, the Pope appeared directly above us at his usual window. Thousands of people were now packed in the square, and we had the moving experience of hearing the Pope's blessing repeated in several languages.

It was so hard to tear ourselves away from Rome and its exciting atmosphere, despite being almost killed several times by taxi drivers who careered through the streets in their small Fiat taxis at incredible speeds, rarely appearing to stop at pedestrian crossings!

Valerie arranged for us to fly direct to London on a Saturday afternoon with an estimated time of arrival at 5.30pm which we thought sufficiently early to secure hotel rooms for the night. Unfortunately, the airline office, unknown to us, had changed our booking to a roundabout flight, so it was with some shock we heard the pilot's voice on the intercom saying,

"Flying time to Frankfurt will be..."

The outcome of this was a long break in a cold and windy airport in Germany, finally arriving in London at 10pm.

Undaunted, we rang several hotels from a phone booth at Heathrow Airport, only to be told,

"Sorry, no rooms," over and over again.

Concerned, we stood outside wondering why it should be so difficult. A friendly porter, sensing our predicament, now approached. He told us that we would not find accommodation in London on such a night. Didn't we realise that this was the day of the World Cup Football Final and London was overflowing with international visitors. He suggested that we try and hire a car and drive it westwards into the country areas where we might find a room, or at the worst, we could always sleep in the car! And so, fortunately, we were able to hire the last available car that night at the airport and set out along the road to Windsor. Again, luckily, although it was now well after midnight, we found accommodation in a small hotel there, and very thankful we were to sink into feather mattressed beds. We did not know it then, but we were to travel over three thousand miles around England in that small Morris car before we finally handed it in after a four month period.

Next morning, no worse for our adventure, especially after a good night's sleep and a good old English breakfast, we ventured forth to explore Windsor which we definitely had made no previous plans to visit. It was a glorious morning, bright and sunny, with an invigorating nip in the air.

"Oh to be in England, now that April's there!" I thought whimsically. Of course, it was June, but it felt really springlike. We loved little Windsor. A great treat was witnessing the changing of the guard at the Castle which coincided with our arrival there. Proud, patriotic feelings swept over me as we toured the chapel, the gardens and parts of the castle. It was a lovely introduction to England which I was pleased to see Val and Elaine enjoying so much.

As we were now in the south-west, we decided to carry on visiting friends and relatives in the southern areas; Horsham, Brighton, Southsea, Poole, Weymouth, Blandford, Exeter, Yeovil. At some of these places we attempted to find accommodation and jobs, but if we discovered one, we were unsuccessful with the other. Frustrated, we halted at Odcombe in Somerset, my parent's home. They were away on holiday but we were able to settle in and gather our thoughts for a few days.

Before they returned we drove northwards to Bath, Bristol, Gloucestershire, Derby and on to Yorkshire where many of our farming relatives lived. Once again we met up with problems in our search to settle. A short stay in beautiful York also dashed our hopes. Now we returned to London where we were offered many posts, but the claustrophobic accommodation of small flats drove us away. We followed this disappointment next with a second journey to the south and on for a five week stay with my parents. This we spent more as a holiday, driving to all the beautiful spots in Devon, Dorset and Somerset. The weather, however, had become atrociously wet and cold, so these charming counties, not at their best, could not influence us to make one of them our home. On a chilly, drizzly day we visited Lawrence of Arabia's cottage in Dorset. Set amongst rhododendrons, in a wide open spaces environment, it seemed to strike a melancholy note which roused our sympathies. Over the door in a stone panel there was an Arabic inscription which we were informed meant "Nothing matters". How unhappy he must have been, and how he must have missed his stimulating former life in the desert sunshine. As we returned to the car, the girls said,

"Let's go home Mum".

Home meaning, of course, Africa.

Maybe it was too early for us to settle away from our beloved Kenya; maybe it was not meant to be, for all our attempts had certainly been frustrated. Next morning as I arose I agreed,

"Alright girls, we'll go back."

Anxious parents waved us off from their home a few days later. Ironically the sun came out for the first time in weeks. It was now late September and as we drove to London we saw farmers cutting their golden corn; it all looked so calm and beautiful and I felt misgivings about our decision which I voiced.

The girls comforted me saying,

"Oh no Mum! Don't worry, we want to go back. We don't feel at home here and everything will be alright. Just you wait and see."

I looked at them then, realising that I had dragged them to two other countries they did not know. They were small children when they went to Kenya and so, of course, Kenya, to them was 'home', where they felt happy and secure in the familiar surroundings.

Someone above was taking care of us as we walked out of Nairobi Airport the following day. A friend, Peter Evans, who was Personnel Officer in the Government, was walking towards us.

"Good gracious!" he exclaimed, "What are you doing here? I thought you had left."

"We did," I laughed, "but we decided to come back. It was so difficult to settle in the UK. "

He looked concerned as he asked,

"What are you going to do now then?"

"I really have no idea," I replied, "I just hope something will work out."

"Come and see me tomorrow morning if you are interested. I have two secretarial posts vacant and there's a house with the jobs out at Kabete."

We could have hugged him. Dear Peter. As we thanked him he grinned and said,

"I guess I was meant to run into you wanderers today!"

What a difference to our experiences in England. We felt now that we had really come 'home'.

CHAPTER TWENTY FIVE

THE START OF A SIX YEAR REPRIEVE

Maureen, of course, was delighted to have us back and in no way disappointed that she would not be joining us in another country. The worst blow was to hear, that in our absence, Sacunda had finally yielded to his advanced years and had reluctantly gone home to Kilimanjaro. We were most upset not to see him, and especially over the coming years, for we were never to meet again.

Elaine and Val secured the promised posts at the Kabete Veterinary Laboratories and very quickly we were installed in a pretty little cottage in the boma there. It was set in a wonderful garden. Some previous employee, we were told, had spent all her spare time developing this and we were benefiting from her labour of love. It was a comforting spot, calming one's fears and anxieties, and brought to mind an extract from an old poem:

"... You are closer to God in a garden than anywhere else on earth."

Our first night, however, was not without some fear. As we sank into our beds after a tiring unpacking, we heard a drunken African staggering up the lane who stopped at our garden hedge. He was shouting abusively, threatening all white people that they would be killed. We sat up, shocked and disturbed, all of us wondering if we should really have returned. The security situation had faded from our minds somewhat during our stay in England, and now here we were on our first night already having doubts and misgivings about our personal safety. Suddenly there was a loud crash and a yell. The African had fallen into a deep ditch by the hedge, where he lay all night, occasionally mumbling or giving the odd belligerent shout. We had very little sleep that night, but at dawn when we ventured out, we found that he had gone. We discovered from the neighbours that he was an old man, a little 'soft' in the head, who was really quite harmless. We lived in the little house at Kabete for two and a half years and regularly each month we heard him blasting forth, but were able to turn over and go to sleep with no worries, although we knew that he often spent the night in our ditch!

The Kabete Veterinary establishment was a friendly place with multi-racial employees, including visiting two year contract veterinary surgeons of German and Canadian origin. There was a Sports Club for the staff where they could play tennis and attend socials, so the days passed by pleasantly enough.

As Maureen's contract with Kenya Television ended, she decided to set herself up as a free lance film editor. Joan and Alan Root, who by this time had become internationally famous for their wild life films, gave her their editing. John Pearson, another well known cameraman, also brought along his work, so she was busy and excited in this new sphere. John Pearson was tragically shot whilst camping in Tanzania in later years, a sad end to a very promising career. All these people spent many hours at our home when in from their filming safaris, and in Maureen's studio we were able to pass opinions on various shots, which I think they valued as we, after all, represented their viewing public. We were proud to be associated with their work, and always look back with admiration of their talents and dedicated study of all wild life.

Lawrence Sagini was glad to see us back. Of course, by now, he had a new secretary, but we often met and also visited his home. I had to sally forth and find new employment which I was fortunate to find with Sir Ernest Vasey. I was to stay with him for several years. He was a lively and kind person who had led a full and interesting life, and was still very active, although in his seventies. Apart from being financial adviser to a group of industrial millionaires, he was also chairman of several other large companies, and a World Bank representative. Earlier in life, he had been Minister for Finance for the Kenyan and Tanzanian Governments, and had also done a spell in Bangladesh, I believe for the World Bank. So my days became hectic and exhilarating as I came in contact with interesting, successful people both internationally and in Kenya.

Valerie renewed a relationship with a former boy friend who lived on an isolated farm at Timau in the shadow of Mount Kenya. We were all invited up there many weekends when the time passed only too quickly. He grew very large areas of wheat, very successfully, and lived in a charming, rustic, timber house which he had designed and built. There we could relax far from the madding crowd. The views were immense, breathtaking at dawn and sunset, and the evenings spent round a large log fire still linger in the memory. Unfortunately, the time came along when his farm was taken over by the Kenya Government. He was compensated, and had to move along. How heartbreaking it was for all the Kenya farmers who had to leave their lives' work in those days, and even now I'm sure they still feel lost and uprooted.

We had other friends at a farm at Naro Moru, again near Mount Kenya, called "Carissa", where we visited regularly. The rambling old house was truly 'Old England', with leaded windows, tall chimneys and shingled roof. The rooms had high, raftered ceilings, and there was even a minstrel's gallery in the enormous lounge. A trout stream meandered through the grounds where it was possible to fish successfully for one's breakfast or evening meal. This house had been built for Mr. Sherbrooke-Walker, the instigator of the famous 'Treetops' tourist attraction in Kenya. Scenes for the film 'Born Free' were also shot here and the film company's crew accommodated in the house.

During the day we would go horse riding, or walk for miles in the bracing country air, and later look in on the evening milking hour. Some of the more energetic types would arrange to climb Mount Kenya, or go shooting on the slopes of the mountain with a hunter who was a regular visitor. Evenings there, after a superb dinner, again round a log fire as we listened to light classical music, will forever stay with us. We became quite nonchalant about driving long distances for these escapes from city life, and never wearied on the journeys, for this, to us, was the real Kenya.

One weekend, along with a friend, we paid a visit to Samburu Lodge, way up in northern Kenya, beyond Isiolo. From Nanyuki onwards, the road was shocking, and as our vehicle was a Cortina car when really we needed a landrover, we had many anxious moments, but the tough little car got us through safely. A breakdown would not have been pleasant in that lonely and very hot area. Nowadays, there is a splendid tar sealed highway running through from Kenya to Ethiopia.

Samburu was an exciting new game lodge on the banks of the Uaso Nyiro River. We saw crocodiles, hippos, and elephants all at very close range. Small squirrels and gaudy birds joined us in the gardens, and cheeky monkeys jumped around in the trees and onto the verandah tables and chairs. On the journey in, we had seen our first gerenuk. Returning to our chalet on the bank of the river one evening, after dark, we heard loud thumps and rustlings, and could vaguely see large forms ambling around. We thought they must be elephants, but they turned out to be hippos which had left the water for an evening's frolic.

We all knew, that gradually, the Kenya Government's aim was to train Africans to take over from the immigrant races of Kenya, so soon the days of Work Permits for non-citizens arrived. We had the choice of becoming Kenya citizens, or relying on two year work permits being renewed. We decided to retain our British citizenship, because we felt that in the long term, the majority of jobs would naturally be given to Africans, and that gradually the white people in Kenya might not be able to secure employment, citizenship or no. Thus, in a country with no social services, we could become involved in a serious financial situation. Most whites in good posts felt they could expect work permits for several years, and in the event such was the case.

We carried on as usual until the time arrived when the government posts at the Veterinary Laboratories were Africanised. Sadly then the girls had to leave and we lost our little house at Kabete. We moved into a flat in Nairobi and soon re-arranged our lives. Elaine obtained a post with the British High Commission, and Val returned to the publicity office at 20th Century Fox Films. Both, very happily, were soon content in their new positions.

Visits up-country still continued, including some to farms at Rongai and Lumbwa. We suffered with the owners as these farms, each in turn, were taken over; the one at Rongai very suddenly, when the owner was unaware as he was away on a visit to Nairobi. He found the farm handed over by Kenyatta to the African employees. The Lumbwa property was owned by a widowed German countess in her seventies. She moved into the Norfolk Hotel in Nairobi to end her days there. These large farms and so many others, in the main, were split up into five acre blocks and given to Africans. Unfortunately, this gradually caused great and serious deterioration in the country's agricultural economy.

The Countess' manager, now unemployed, was offered a post running a tea estate at Tinderet which he took out of sheer necessity, although he had no experience of this kind. He and his wife invited us there for a long weekend. How they ever got in or out of the place in the rainy seasons we'll never know. The drive in on a ghastly track, or no road at all, up and down rocky hills and crags, through wooded valleys which never dried out, was a nightmare to us. The views, however, from the hill tops were fantastic, where one looked out over a fabulous panorama, which included Lake Victoria.

On arrival, the sight of thousands of rows of neat tea bushes, the shining white factory and the welcoming cup of tea in their comfortable home was sufficient reward for the tough journey. It was very cold up there at high altitude, and the mist came down in the early evenings and lingered on in the mornings giving it all an eerie stillness. John proudly escorted us round the factory of which he was now in charge. The girls fired questions at him as to what this, that, and the other was for, until John had to break in and say,

"Girls, girls! What I know about tea at this stage, is positively dangerous!"

A great humorist always, he luckily had a helpful and competent staff!

Several other weekends were spent at our beloved coast. The 350 mile journey gradually became easier as overseas aid helped the Kenya Government to build a tar sealed road, but we looked back nostalgically on our real safari days of flooded rifts, skiddy areas or choking dust, and the friendly stops at dukas and hotels. Now one pressed on with perhaps just one break and some of the old adventurous stimulation was sadly missing. At the coast itself, the erection of the first large tourist hotels, needed to boost the country's sagging economy, was to us, an unwelcome scar on the natural beauty of the coastline.

The political scene was peaceful on the surface, but there was a strong undercurrent of tribal jealousies and discontent. The Kikuyus held most of the high positions. The Vice-President was a Jaluo. Thought to be too powerful after a disastrous visit to Kisumu by Kenyatta to open a new hospital there, he was whisked away into detention. Unfortunately, several promising Ministers and other politicians died as a result of mysterious road accidents. Others were voted out at suspected rigged elections. Tom Mboya, also a Jaluo, a Minister dedicated to the economic future of Kenya, a brilliant young man, was eyed with suspicion by the Kikuyu.

Armed robbery of houses and factories, bank robberies, car theft and rape of white women were everyday occurrences. When revelling in our country visits, or at the coast in magnificent Kenya, we dismissed these unpleasant happenings from our minds. After a weekend at Rongai, Lumbwa or Tinderet, we would stay on as long as possible, rising at 4 am on the Monday mornings to drive all the way into Nairobi and go straight to our working desks. It would be dark and cold at first, but then as we crossed the floor of the Great Rift Valley, the sun would slowly and majestically rise over the escarpment; the animals and birds all came to life; sometimes a stately giraffe would saunter across the road or a few small buck joyously bound through the near undergrowth. We would stop for a cup of tea and a sandwich, a breakfast provided by our host, drinking in also the enthralling beauty and activity around us.

Despite the country's instability, how could we ever bear to leave all this for another world!

CHAPTER TWENTY SIX

EVENTFUL DAYS

We were surprised one day by a lady of the church begging us to join the choir at the cathedral. Apparently the number of choir members had become sadly depleted. Like John, with his tea, we felt that what we knew about music was also dangerous, and although we could possibly sing in key, we knew that we did not possess good voices.

"It doesn't matter. We desperately need people to help swell the volume. We already have good voices to lead. Please come and help, if only for a short time," she pleaded.

She was very persistent and so we found ourselves attending choir practices and singing at the services on Sundays which curtailed our up-country visits somewhat. However, we became involved and began to take a real interest in music. It was a very good choir and when a tape was made of us singing the Hallelujah Chorus we could not believe we were part of that pleasing professional sound. We also took part in many happy social outings with members of the choir, thus enlarging our circle of friends.

Our saddest task in the choir days was after one bleak Saturday when Tom Mboya, the Jaluo Minister, was gunned down by an assassin as he stepped out of a chemist's shop in Nairobi. He died on the way to hospital. What a tragic end to a brilliant young man's career who could have contributed a great deal to Kenya in the years ahead. The choir was ordered to sing at his funeral. My employer, Sir Ernest, advised us not to go.

"There will be trouble," he warned.

I thought long and hard about this as I knew the Jaluo tribe believed that the Kikuyu had planned to kill Tom Mboya and were seething with hatred and revenge. But, I had known Tom Mboya personally, in the working area, and put that first. Yes, I would sing at his funeral. The girls agreed that they would also like to be there. On the day we had difficulty in reaching the cathedral. Thousands of Africans teemed round the church; soldiers and police struggled to maintain order. I had already decided to park our car far away. Finally, with the help of the police, we were able to fight our way through the frightening mob and reach our seats in the church, but not without some apprehension. Once inside, however, we felt safe and pleased that we had come. The floral tributes were overwhelming; the coffin lying in state on the altar surrounded by these, the aisles and every inch of available space still insufficient to take these offerings to a lost and respected African.

We watched as the invited congregation gathered; family, friends, ambassadors, Ministers and civil servants. Television cameras were placed in suitable positions, one near the great door. Now we just awaited the arrival of the President and his wife. Suddenly, a moment of terror, as we saw through the open door that thousands of Africans were surging towards the building, shouting, screaming and gesticulating as the President's car neared the entrance. We were told later that this had been held up and stoned. Val now whispered,

"What's all that smoke?"

The 'smoke' wafted through the open door and we quickly discovered that it was tear gas. The President and his wife were rushed in, the great doors slammed, but not before a ridiculous vision of the cameraman and his video machine being hastily pushed outside to achieve this. Now came an ominous silence as the police successfully turned away the mob.

Our eyes streaming with tears, our throats dry and burned, we witnessed the President being given a glass of water. We panicked a little as more tear gas drifted in through slit windows which were not glazed. The mob surged backwards and forwards, some of them at times reaching the doors when they tried to batter their way in.

"Oh God!" I prayed, "please take care of us all."

Looking up, I now saw the Archbishop, an elderly gentleman, calmly commencing the service. How could he manage to speak, how could we possibly sing, but we did! The noise outside continued to recede and return at regular intervals. I saw a group of nuns completely oblivious of everything except their devotion to this moving burial service, and I whispered to the girls that we should try and follow their example.

As the service neared its conclusion, security officers and bodyguards anxiously peered from windows and visited a side door regularly. The Archbishop then informed us that the President's party would leave first by this side door when there was a suitable lull in the outside activity. Then, he said, the same would apply for us all to leave in groups. In the meantime we were to remain seated.

As Kenyatta and his wife left, I realised that the mob had indeed been driven very well away and that there was no sound of their immediate return. As we were seated only a few yards from the door, I quietly beckoned the girls to follow me.

"Come quickly, we will also go now. Run like mad for the back streets and the car."

We were not deterred, but what a horrible sight everywhere; thousands of rocks, shoes and other missiles littered the ground; an old Sikh propped by the cathedral wall, obviously dead. We did not stop, as in the distance we could hear the howling mob returning, but not in the direction we were taking. I was so thankful we got away at this time, for in their frustration at Jomo Kenyatta escaping them, the mob later tore through Nairobi, smashing shop windows, turning over motor cars, pillaging, and anyone in the way was an easy target for injury.

We reached our car and drove in a safe roundabout way to our flat, but we still saw vehicles in ditches, a landrover upside down across the road, and a car upended on a tree with a dead man still clutching the steering wheel. In a state of shock, and feeling quite ill from the tear gas we had inhaled, we collapsed into chairs at home. Maureen, who had been unable to attend the funeral, owing to a dose of flu, was still gazing at the TV.

"Oh what a beautiful service!" she said, "I do wish I could have gone with you. How he must have been loved. All that huge congregation crying their eyes out!"

We looked at her in amazement.

"Do you mean no one announced what was really happening? Didn't you see all the rioting and tear gas bombs exploding?" we gasped.

"Why no! Do you mean there has been trouble after all?" she worriedly replied.

"My goodness, yes! Most of those tears you saw were from tear gas and we never thought we would get home safely."

After explaining in more detail, and from the state we were in, she tried to help and comfort us and I'm sure was very glad that she had escaped such an ordeal.

It took several days for us to recover from sore eyes, burned throats, noses and stomachs, and so we will never forget Tom Mboya's funeral or the blood curdling, primitive sounds of thousands of Africans protesting and rioting. Next morning, by Government order, there was not a sign of any disturbance in the city. In the hours of darkness, the surroundings of the cathedral and all the streets were meticulously cleaned up. Repairs had been made to shop windows and damaged vehicles removed. Nothing at all to show for our traumatic moments!

Flat life gradually restricted us. We missed the wide open spaces and felt the need to step out into a garden of our own again. Maureen also needed larger studio facilities, so we arranged a further move to a large old settler's house in the Kiambu area, which proved to be our last Kenya home. This was the first house built in that district when the owner purchased the land and planted the first coffee there in the early 1900's.

Security there was better than in Nairobi, so we were not afraid. We had close neighbours, the houses of the estate manager and a doctor being situated at each side of our five acre garden. The coffee factory was also very near where the staff lived alongside in large quarters. Our homes were fitted with battery run sirens in case of trouble, and we had diligent night watchmen, brave Somalis, who patrolled the grounds and manned a barrier at the drive entrance to Anmer Estate. Anmer House had large verandahs on three sides, which were fenced in with strong steel and wire screens, and the enormous double doors at all entrances were drawn and securely padlocked at night. A hanging cord in each room needed only a slight pull to activate the sirens, but this was to cause a few false alarms in our early days. The first night we moved in, Kitonyi, our houseboy, mistook it for the light switch. What a din!

It took me back to war time in England, for the noise was equally as loud as the old air raid sirens and could be heard for miles. One or two of our visitors made the same mistake, which was very embarrassing for us, and a little worrying that we might have called wolf too often, as at each alarm we found the watchmen galloping up madly, the estate manager banging on the back door and all the neighbours ringing up on the telephone to ask what the trouble was. It was comforting to have this quick response. However, thankfully, we never experienced the need to use the sirens in any emergency in our days at Kiambu which were peacefully happy for over three years.

The house commanded magnificent views. From the front verandah we could look straight ahead to Mount Kilimanjaro which gladdened our eyes on many, many mornings and evenings. It could be so startlingly visible in the clear African air, although over one hundred miles away. As we drove down the drive at the back of the house, bound for Nairobi, the sight of Mount Kenya cheered us on our way, again despite being over a hundred miles to the north. Ol Donyo Sabuk, a mere hill in comparison, but still a purple vision, was a welcome side view from the eastern verandah. We had another glorious Kenya garden with brick paved paths leading to a large lily pond and gaudy flower beds. An enclosed rose-garden gave off a heavenly aroma when the three hundred trees flourished and blossomed, which seemed to be perpetually. Jacaranda trees, pine trees, and brilliant flame trees surrounded the house. Native fruit trees and three large avocado pear trees supplied us with healthy fare. All around us on the gentle slopes grew thousands of acres of coffee trees, at seasonal times a blaze of white flowers, or bright red berries. At picking time, hundreds of African bibis could be seen bobbing up and down amongst the trees, their bright head scarves a kaleidoscope of colours. They would be singing, laughing and shouting; a vibrant, exhilarating sound.

So many birds aroused us from our slumbers at the dawn of each day, the trees and shrubs full of them. The lawns were sometimes a carpet of vividly coloured superb starlings. Swallows nested in the rafters of the high verandahs, returning each year. They sat on the verandah chairs, flew in and out of the lounge through the open doors and windows, making themselves really at home. They were so tame and gave us great pleasure. So many places in the world have been described as an Eden; this surely must have been one of them. All the misgivings and fears regarding Kenya's difficult years were forgotten, when home from work we could relax in this paradise. Our many friends in Nairobi would drive out at weekends to enjoy it all with us, and very loath they were to leave at the end of the day.

The profound beauty of the area stirred my creative instincts. I had had some success as an artist in my youth, but over the busy family years had laid aside my brushes; now I was inspired to try again. All my spare moments were spent on the verandah or out in the country, trying to bring to life on paper and canvas, all the scenes around me. I was grateful for this gift which now filled my life.

Maureen's talents were also being tested by the editing of films for Joan and Alan Root, such as "Mzima Springs" and "Baobab", which were to grace the television screens of the world. We were privileged to have private viewings of these films at home and be able to pass on our comments. Elaine was well established at the British High Commission. The invites she received to various functions often included members of her family, so we met many visitors to Kenya, including Prince Charles and Princess Anne.

Val was to meet her fate in these early Kiambu days. Hugh was not sure about their future in Kenya and wished to choose a new country of abode, so he went off to Europe and America to look round. However, on return, he had decided to forget those areas and emigrate to Australia. I was glad for Val as they made their plans to marry and use the boat trip to Australia as their honeymoon, but also very sad at the thought of their impending departure. Like any mother, breaking the ties of so many years was hard to bear, and I wished they could stay nearby. Common sense had to prevail, as I knew there was no real future for the young white people of Kenya, and as Val said and hoped, we would probably follow them.

We had all kept a brave face at the wedding and later in Nairobi as we saw them off at the station. Val, excited and happy until the last moment, suddenly realised she was leaving us and her beloved Kenya, and burst into anguished tears. Of course, we were soon in the same state, but gradually managed to comfort each other until she boarded the train in happier mood. We were not sure then that we would all live in Australia one day, but fate had her own ideas on the matter as time would tell.

We missed Val so much. Her vacant bedroom brought a lump to my throat each time I passed the door. Letters from Australia disturbed me. They had reached the city of Perth in the middle of its very hot summer, which to a newcomer unaccustomed to such heat, can be a shattering experience. Were they going to like it, be happy there and able to settle? Eventually the letters became more reassuring and I felt content.

To relieve the sad, quieter atmosphere at home, I agreed to have the elderly mother of a doctor friend stay with us for one month whilst he and his family took an overseas holiday. She had been unlucky to go down with cerebral malaria whilst living in the Congo in earlier years, and although able to get around famously physically, she was rather absent minded and lived in a little world of her own. Still on medication which kept her happy, we found we had no trouble at all. She was a sweet lady and seemed to take to the Kiambu surroundings so well, that when it was time for her to go home, she pleaded to stay a little longer. The days grew into weeks, the weeks to months, and eventually after a year we managed to persuade her to return home!

Her stay had its amusing moments, tinged with danger. Coming through for dinner one evening from her guest wing, she dreamily announced that there had been a big black dudu (insect) in her room earlier in the day. She thought it had gone now! As we had a dinner guest, and as dudus were so prevalent in Kenya, her remark slipped from our minds as we wined and dined and spent a pleasant evening. At 11pm we started the usual nightly security checks. Finally returning to the dining room, and looking in from the French windows, we were startled to see a large tarantula spider clinging to the picture rail in the far corner of the room. Assuredly, this must be Mrs. Babault's dudu! None of us was brave enough to tackle such a formidable creature and yet we knew we could not settle for the night with it around. Muthaika and Kitonyi had long gone to their quarters, but we decided to rouse them and ask for their help. As they peered in at the offensive intruder exclaiming,

"Mbaya sana Memsahib, hii sumu sana, kali kabisa!" (It is very bad madam, very poisonous and very savage) we thought that they too were not keen on any onslaught. However, Muthaika disappeared, returning with the kitchen mop from which he removed the head. Stepping into the room he asked us to close the door behind him. What cowards we felt shuddering out there on the verandah. He stood for quite a time eyeing the spider; the spider watching him with equal intensity. Then he slowly raised the mop handle, carefully aiming it as a spear. We thought he would never throw it, but suddenly it flew through the air at lightning speed. The spider fell to the ground; Muthaika dashed over and gave it an almighty wallop, after which he turned and grinned at us triumphantly.

On viewing the body we saw that one leg was lying apart, and he explained that he had taken a long time to throw his makeshift spear as he needed to be sure that he would break at least one leg so that when it fell to the ground it would be unable to move and attack him. Muthaika was part Masai, so obviously his inherent hunting instincts and dexterity with a spear relieved us of an unwelcome visitor on that night.

The next adventure came when Mrs. Babault again announced that there was something in her bathroom, but the electric bulb had gone and she could not see what it was. She said she had tried to drive it out with the lavatory brush! Kitonyi went through to replace the electric bulb. Unbelievably, as light returned, he found a young spitting cobra there, quite at home in its new surroundings. We heard yells and thumps and quickly rushed to find him depositing its dead body on the verandah. Later, he and Muthaika took it some distance from the house and buried it, in order to discourage any visit from its searching parent. We were aware that the thick mulch which was placed round the coffee trees was a favourite haunt of many cobras. We were indeed grateful that Mrs. Babault escaped harm from these unpleasant intruders.

CHAPTER TWENTY SEVEN

ANMER HOUSE

After Mrs. Babault's departure, a change in my working life was to take place. The hectic pace of trying to keep up with so many affairs had taken its toll and I had a period of ill health. A white hunter we knew asked if I would like to run his small office instead.

"Take things easier," he said, "have a change from all that intense stuff, do something more relaxing and entertaining!"

Entertaining it certainly proved to be, relaxing, hardly!

I was whisked into a life of meeting wealthy international clients, haunting the game department for licences to shoot certain animals, and helping to organise the various safaris. Getting a safari on the road was an Herculean task of packing all the necessary gear; tents, furniture, bedding, fridges, portable bathrooms, cookers, table linen, guns, ammunition etc., etc. Then, of course, there was the food. The clients expected gourmet dishes as our brochures promised. This all had to be calculated and packed in deep freezers; turkeys, chickens, ducks, prawns, lobsters, the best of fruit and vegetables and so much more. Drinks, including expensive wines, spirits, beer, and soft drinks, also ice. I dreamed of food in the days preceding a safari. Once I had the horrible shock of a radio call informing me that the truck had broken down halfway to the rendezvous and that the food was all spoiled. Would I arrange for a light aircraft to fly out another consignment plus spares for the vehicle!

Each time the convoy drove away on safari I breathed a sigh of relief as I knew I then had three weeks or so to catch up on office work and arrange for the next influx of customers. In this period of time, a duplicate set of equipment was also prepared; tents and mosquito nets repaired, furniture cleaned and painted if necessary, blankets and linen laundered. Previous hunting trophies had to be checked at the taxidermists and transportation to America, England, France, Germany or Japan verified. The stuffed head of a greater kudu stood on my office floor once for over three weeks. Each time I sat at my desk, its sad, mournful eyes reproached and haunted me.

"Don't you ever dare to leave another one like that in my office," I also reproached my boss on his return!

The office was reminiscent of a curio shop, decorated with spears, poisoned arrows, carvings, stuffed heads, rugs made from various animal skins, shields and many other items collected over the years. The clients lapped up this atmosphere and returned regularly for further safaris.

An incoming safari provided a pleasant lull when Tony did his best to appease my tattered nerves. I was always included in farewell parties for the clients in the luxurious hotels of Nairobi, and he also took me out for lunches in between his amorous adventures with very beautiful girls. A good looking man, he was never short of companions; I can truthfully say he was the epitome of the much publicised romantic white hunter. Despite the stressful moments and great activity, I really enjoyed my year with him, at the end of which I had to seek further employment as work permits were now only being granted for positions in government offices or at embassies.

I was lucky to become Secretary to the Head of the British Council in Nairobi. Bob Hack, my new boss, had a quiet, kind, soothing personality, so these days I remember as peaceful and happy ones. I discovered the great range of activities covered by the Council and the efficient way they were carried out. We had quite a large staff to deal with the sizeable library, the film and music department, the educational and scholarship department, the accounts and the V.S.O's who came out from England. These V.S.O's had many experiences, some traumatic, such as when they all had to be rounded up safely from the horrific state of Uganda in the days of Idi Amin. Visiting professional people who came out to lecture at the university and hospitals all had to be taken care of, and their itineraries prepared, so the days were full and very interesting. Social affairs, chiefly cocktail parties, were regularly attended, sometimes almost to the point of tedium, but in my future life of less exhilarating days I would have given anything for their return.

Since our arrival at Kiambu we had been friendly with a widow and her grown up daughter who lived on an adjacent coffee estate. The mother, alone on the estate during Mau Mau days, had many grisly tales to tell. She was one of the tough old characters of Kenya who also had a heart of gold if one was in trouble. She missed her husband dreadfully and could become very depressed on occasions, thus becoming vulnerable to suggestions from spiritualists who promised her comfort. Once she told me that a ghost haunted her home regularly, which she said was an elderly lady relative of the family. On weekends when her daughter sometimes went away, Beatrice would beg me to sleep at her home for company. I gave in on a few occasions, but never happily, as I would be installed in a guest wing of the house, far from her cosy bedroom upstairs. All night long I would jump at the slightest noise, or become terrified by a night watchman on his rounds who would flash his torch in the outside gardens, thus causing eerie reflections on my bedroom window.

The house could certainly have been a ghost's paradise. Approaching it up a long drive through neglected park land, one could imagine oneself in the deep south of America, as it greatly resembled the old cotton plantation homes there, with its pillared verandahs and architectural design. Stepping into the large panelled lounge, from which a wooden staircase ascended, it was decidedly creepy, as the dark wooden walls greatly diminished any incoming light from the small windows! The walls of the lounge and staircase were adorned with the stuffed heads of all the species of animals in Africa, even a rhinoceros of no mean size! Never at all fond of this type of decor, I could not bear to look at so many accusing eyes. Beatrice was not particularly happy with them, but explained that her father-in-law had shot them all and they were already installed when she came to the house as a bride. She had once tried to sell them but there were no takers!

In the Mau Mau days Beatrice had one experience which proved to be tragic for her staff, but coupled with that was a rather humorous albeit humane aspect. She retired to bed one night when she heard many birds shrieking and squawking outside the window. They were flapping their wings, banging the window panes and appeared to have gone crazy. On looking out she found that the swallows' nests under the eaves of the house, wherein nestled a great many baby swallows, had all been infested with safari ants. Their agitated parents were flying round and round and doing anything in an attempt to scare them away, uselessly of course. Beatrice went off to rouse her house servants, telling them to bring ladders and gloves. The Africans climbed up and collected the baby swallows which they handed in baskets to Beatrice through the nearest bedroom windows. She then proceeded to try and save them. Some died, already devoured or too badly bitten, but the others she valiantly dealt with all night long.

Around dawn, completely exhausted, she walked out on her front verandah. She saw a European police inspector and several African askaris coming up the drive. The inspector appeared to be very agitated and in a very annoyed tone shouted,

"What the hell are you doing outside madam? Why haven't you set off the alarms? What's wrong with you?"

Perplexed and amazed at his manner she spluttered,

"I've been saving baby swallows."

Looking at her now, as if she was out of her mind, he told her there was a dead African girl at the end of her drive and that the Mau Mau had raided the farm labourers' camp, wounding several of them. They had come to get the girl who they said was a police informer. They had dragged her from the camp past the end of Beatrice's house and all the way down the drive where they killed her and went off. Beatrice almost collapsed as she had never heard a sound.

After arranging necessary help for the inspector she felt some delayed shock and great concern for her staff. The inspector hardly comforted her with his last rather sarcastic comment as he left,

"I'm so pleased you managed to save some birds madam!"

Lighter relief came one evening when we found we had no water in the house, and we had to seek help from Jim, the estate manager. The pump house was in a paddock beyond our garden fence; the road to the paddock was a roundabout track of some distance through the coffee. In jocular mood, Jim said that he would jump over our fence in order to save his legs. We watched as he athletically vaulted over and safely reached the pump house. It was a bright moonlight night and he was soon shouting that all was well. Grateful, we shouted back that he should come and have a drink with us for his trouble. He was halfway back when we heard a threatening bellow.

"My God!" Jim yelled. "I forgot, the men put the bull in here today!"

I have never seen anyone run so fast; he threw himself over our hedge just in time to miss the deadly horns of a very large and irate animal.

A scary episode occurred at Anmer House when Maureen suddenly found some African women breaking down one of our 6 foot high hedges with their pangas in order to clamber up some custard apple trees to collect the fruit. They had made a terrible mess. She ran across the lawn shouting at them to stop and to come to the house if they wanted some fruit. Whereupon one of them advanced towards her, waving her panga and shouting,

"They are not your trees. It's not your fruit. It belongs to the Africans."

She meant business!

Luckily Muthaika heard the din from the kitchen and dashed out with a rungu (a club with a very heavy wooden knob at the end). He grabbed Maureen just in time and got her safely back to the house. They were both shaken and were trembling. The African women ran off, somewhat scared now they knew our staff were around. Muthaika then told Maureen never to be so foolhardy again as to try and deal alone with a group of hostile Kikuyu women.

"They would have killed you!" he said.

Again more white people were leaving the country now that the work permit situation was tightening up. Dangerous security problems ebbed and flowed. Whites were being attacked, sometimes at night as they reached their homes. A gang would be waiting in the garage ready to pounce on them the moment they alighted from their car. Some were killed. Another trick at night, on lonely roads, was for one car load of Africans to follow an isolated vehicle, whilst way ahead there would be another car of associates waiting. As the victims approached the waiting car it would move out and block the road. The one behind would come up, cutting off any hope of escape. So the people were robbed, beaten up and the women sometimes raped. If only one person was in the car, they might be left in the boot all night, or until someone heard their cries for help. We rarely ventured out at night except to close neighbours' homes, but managed to keep a comfortable social life going this way.

Independence had not achieved a peaceful situation. Tribal jealousies became more and more apparent. A new society was emerging of politicians and businessmen who were searching for some kind of identity that could not be dubbed 'capitalist'. Poverty increased and with it, theft. Gangs roamed the towns holding up people in shops, restaurants and bars at gun point. People in Nairobi became alarmed locking themselves in their homes behind barred doors and windows at night. They installed alarm systems and hired night watchmen.

Rebelling against this prolonged lifestyle, Maureen and Allison, Beatrice's daughter, conspired together to bring back a little of the former gaiety of Kenya. They decided to hold a party for at least two hundred people. We were sceptical of the success of such a party as the invitations went out to people of all areas in Kenya. We also hoped that they could cater for such a party if the invitations were all accepted! However, they were very determined young ladies and soon announced that the menu was organised. All from the farm, sheep would be slaughtered for mutton curry; turkeys, chickens and ducks would be prepared for the cold collations, and as there was plenty of cream, butter and cheese and all the fruit and vegetables in the gardens, it was easy! Guests would be asked to bring their own drinks. The venue would be Beatrice's home, and the neighbours all agreed that our staffs would help out on the day. The disco craze had just caught on in Nairobi in those days, so the best group from town was booked. And so, they informed us, all was ready!

The invitations, amazingly, were all accepted, some of the guests travelling two and three hundred miles, and what a magical night it proved to be. I was over at the house earlier in the day when I thought how impossible it seemed that everything would be ready in time. The outside kitchen was something to behold; the old cook in charge, shouting to his many bewildered helpers, who for lack of space were just falling over each other. Huge sufurias (pans) of mutton curry were simmering on the stoves; the pet parrot was flying loose, cackling, chattering and landing on the edge of cooking pots where he took it upon himself to be chief taster; pet lambs huddled on sacks near a stove, refusing to move, their plaintive bleats adding to the commotion; the farm dogs dashing in and out, determined not to miss out on any tasty morsels that might be going. Hygiene was hardly the first consideration, but despite all, the food was ready in time, and it all tasted delicious!

The "Bush Telegraph" had been working for days, and the local Africans gathered round the house, not wishing to miss any of the fun and frolics. Some acted as efficient car park attendants as the many visitors arrived. The disco music blared forth deafeningly, the flashing coloured lights dazzling one and all. The gathering that night was a blessed tonic for the tired, anxious Europeans who relaxed, reminisced and met up with friends they had not seen for months, or even years, and were given fresh heart to carry on. Most of them did not leave until dawn. The Africans enjoyed it immensely. We could see large crowds of them at the far side of the lawns, clapping, dancing and singing. Boys from the coffee estates, bibis, old people and children were all there. They, too, did not go short of treats from the kitchen where they made frequent visits. Seated on the front verandah at one stage, I was amused to see black hands creeping round the edge of hessian curtains which had been hung round the drinks bar. They would snatch the first bottle they felt, which could be empty, or luckily whisky or beer, and quickly disappear in the darkness.

There were many hangovers next day and not much work could be expected from one's staff, but we did not mind as they had enjoyed themselves along with two hundred white people, and we wished Kenya's problems could only be settled as amicably. They talked of the party for months. Meeting up with the old sub-chief one day, I was surprised to hear him say how much he had enjoyed it.

"Oh! Were you there? I didn't see you all night," I said.

"But of course I was!" he replied. "Someone had to watch over all those gatecrashers!"

"Lakini, hii party mzuri kabisa, kabisa memsahib. Sawa sawa Ray Anthony Show." (But Memsahib, it was a very, very good party, absolutely. Just like the Ray Anthony Show.)

I laughed out loud. What a description!

I knew that a local Indian duka owner had installed a TV in his shop to entice African custom. For buying his goods, he allowed them to stay on watching the magic screen, and obviously the Ray Anthony Show was their favourite programme.

The exhilaration the party instilled in us all, and the chatting over of the amusing incidents of its duration, kept us happy for quite a long period of time.

CHAPTER TWENTY EIGHT

LATTER DAYS AT ANMER

So we went on, a month, two months, three months until something unpleasant would again crop up. Letters from Australia, and from my brother in New Zealand, begging us to get out of Africa, began to have an effect.

There followed more distressing days of armed robbery when isolated farms and coffee estates became the chief targets on pay days. Six or eight Africans in a stolen, powerful engined vehicle would drive up to the farm offices where perhaps only one African clerk would be counting out the money. He would be quickly overpowered, the money snatched, and they would be gone in a flash. The vehicle would be found later abandoned in or near the city. The Managers of the estates tightened up on security, placing guards round the offices, and barriers to deter vehicles. They rotated pay days to try and deceive the thieves, but they must have had terrified inside informers, as they still came on the days the money was there. Undaunted by guards, they still succeeded, for their guns were formidable aids. Europeans no longer carried guns in an independent country and, even if they had, the penalty for killing or maiming an African was too dangerous an action to contemplate. This reign of terror lasted some considerable time before it was controlled and it affected a near neighbour and our own Anmer Estate.

The neighbour, Chris, was sitting in his farm office one afternoon when one of his garden boys ran in telling him that some strangers were coming through the coffee on foot. He feared they might be robbers. Chris quickly told him to rush off through the coffee trees another way and go to the next farm to tell the bwana there to ring the police and also to come and help. He then looked out to see if he could reach his house which was close by, as his small son, only two years of age, was having his afternoon nap there. His wife had gone into town to do some shopping. It was too late; the gang was upon him. They pushed him inside and told him to open the safe. He said he didn't have the key and there was no money in the safe anyway.

One of them said,

"Kill him!"

They were armed, so reluctantly he got out the keys. Pretending he didn't know the right one he kept trying them one by one to play for time but they grabbed him, snatched the keys, opened the safe and took the money. Then they tied him up and tore the telephone cable from the wall. They now demanded his car key. Fearing for his life and that of his son, he handed over the key and they left. His car was a brand new Saab and he soon heard it roaring away down the drive.

Shortly afterwards his Greek neighbour arrived and released him. He said he had rung the police and also other neighbours. The Greek had been robbed himself the previous month. The police were quick to act that day. They knew there were only two roads out of the estate, so they immediately arranged road blocks at both of them, as they suspected the thieves would steal a car. Sure enough the police askaris soon heard the Saab coming towards them at great speed with both headlights flashing. The thieves had no intention of stopping, so the police opened fire. Two were killed, others wounded and were then arrested. The police found money in the pockets of the two killed with bullet holes through it. However, all the money was not retrieved!

The sequel to this event came when Chris' wife was driving along the same road on her way home and saw her husband's car in the ditch full of bullet holes like the remnant of some gangsters' shoot-out. She almost fainted with fright thinking that her husband and son must have been attacked. How thankful she was to reach home where she found them both safe and sound.

One weekend we paid a visit to "Carissa" and found that our friends who ran the place were packing up to leave. It all seemed so sad. As we roamed the grounds and sat by the trout stream it was hard to accept that it would be our last stay at this beautiful place.

We also longed to see the coast and set off one day to escape from the tense atmosphere of Nairobi. We had been warned that the Masai were now blocking the Mombasa road with their cattle and stopping cars in order to steal, but we decided to risk it; however, we found it to be so. We were very lucky when we had to slow down for such a blockage, as before the Masai reached our car, a truck and two more cars came up behind us and the Masai decided to move their cattle so we could pass through safely. Our lovely coastline by now had changed to a huge tourist stronghold. So many large hotels stretched for miles both north and south of Mombasa. It was difficult for local people to book a room and we had to pay heavily for the pleasure. The old graceful dining room meals served to one at tables were a thing of the past. It was all self-service buffet meals with tourists grabbing food as if they had not eaten for a week. I guess they wanted the most for their money, but it all seemed rather distasteful to us.

During our stay we visited an old friend, Peter, in Mombasa. He was a retired schoolteacher who had a lovely house at Likoni. He had managed very well for years with an old servant who cared for all his needs. We found a new African greeting us and later serving us at dinner. Peter told us that the old one had left him to go and work in a tourist hotel in Malindi. Peter had been dismayed at his abandonment but the old boy was determined to go.

"For the money," he said. Peter offered to pay him more but the old one said he wouldn't be able to give him enough; in Malindi he said he could get £5 every morning plus his salary.

"£5 every morning, whatever for?" Peter exclaimed.

"Well Bwana, all my friends have gone there and they say that when they take the morning tea in for the lady tourists, if there is a £5 note on the bedside table, it means that you have to get into bed with the lady. So my friends get into bed every morning and they are making lots of money," he replied.

Peter could not dissuade him by pointing out that he was no longer a young man and off he went. Some months later however, we heard he had returned to Peter saying he couldn't stand the pace!

We returned safely from the coast in convoy. A very unhappy and subdued Muthaika now told us that his wife had run away and could he have leave to go and find her. He had found a replacement to carry out his duties so we let him go. We missed his chocolate cakes and scones on Sunday tea times and so did our visitors for he was a good cook. Weeks went by and he did not return. Kitonyi worried as they were great friends, but he never did return.

Joseph, our gardener, was married to a very young girl. She already had one child and was pregnant again. One Saturday she had a false alarm and we got the ambulance to take her to Kiambu hospital (a costly business) but she came home next day. Eventually when she started with the genuine labour pains, Joseph came to the house to say he was frightened and handed us a letter from the Kiambu hospital to say she had to return there for a caesarean operation when the baby was due. She had been given this when she left there on her first visit but they had never told us. We rang for the ambulance immediately but when it came she refused to go. In despair we all begged her to agree but she was hysterical. The ambulance driver shrugged and asked for the money. Now an old African midwife appeared and took the girl inside calming her down into silence. The ambulance driver wanted to leave as he said he could not wait; the hospital was very busy and he would get into trouble. We went into the house to try and convince her that she must go but to our horror saw her kneeling on the floor already producing the baby before our eyes. We again said it would be better to go so that she had good care but to no avail. Now we had to pay for the ambulance! Next morning she was out in the garden hanging out her washing, bright as a button! Joseph then came to ask for an advance so that he could buy towels and other necessities for the baby. We handed over the money, only to find a short time later that he had returned, not with towels, but with beer! All our staff and the staff from next door then imbibed themselves useless in order to celebrate the birth.

Maintenance of public health services was now sadly deteriorating and cholera injections became necessary when there were two outbreaks of cholera in and around Nairobi and one at Kisumu. We went to see our Italian friend, Dr. Landra, for these. He told us that if there was an outbreak in our district we must "Keepa the cook outa the kitchen!" One day Kitonyi said a friend of Muthaika's had arrived at the quarters. He was very sick and wanted to sleep in Muthaika's room; could he have the key. We found him very sick indeed with what could have been cholera, so we very quickly paid once again for the ambulance to whisk him away. We advised our staff to clean and disinfect anything he may have touched or used.

We took a further short break at Naivasha where Alan and Joan

Root had bought a property by the lake. We really relaxed and enjoyed seeing their house. Maureen was editing a new film for them at the time.

There were quite a few animals in fenced off areas such as the elusive Bongo which was scarce and very difficult to find in Kenya. Crested cranes roamed the lawns. A tame hyena and a cerval cat wandered in and out of the lounge often giving visitors a scare when they shot in and jumped up on their knees. Alan had become very famous by now. He had his own plane which he flew in and out to save time as he was always so busy. We felt that he would be one of the people who would stay on in Africa and be peaceably allowed to carry on with his film work as it was good publicity for the country. He was born in Kenya and had a good rapport with the Africans.

It was difficult for us to contemplate leaving Kenya, but we often discussed it. Then on a beautiful morning, with the birds singing, Kilimanjaro visible and all the flowers and shrubs ablaze in the garden, we could not bear the thought of going.

We suffered with various illnesses. Elaine and I caught viral hepatitis, a depressing and debilitating affliction which took months to overcome. Maureen had a return bout of dysentery. To cheer us up we decided to pay a visit to the cinema to see 'Gone with the Wind' which we thoroughly enjoyed. Afterwards as we reached our car, I was about to open the door when Elaine shouted,

"Look out Mum!"

All I felt was someone snatching my handbag. It was a young boy who shot off like the wind, weaving his way through the parked cars. We gave chase with a few people helping, but he disappeared in the far distance. Elaine remarked that my bag had also "gone with the wind!"

There was a fair amount of money in it, plus my driving licence and several other items of that nature which I knew would be difficult to replace. We went to the police station and I went through two or three hours of making the same old frustrating report. Then I was asked where my car was. They said I could not drive it now as I had no driving licence! However, I got round that one by saying my daughter was covered by insurance to drive it and that she had a driving licence. They did not appear very pleased to hear that. It took many tiring and anxious trips to government offices before I finally replaced all my necessary papers.

Another rather frightening affair concerning driving was that one always had to be on the alert for the sound of sirens. Jomo Kenyatta always had a motorcade of advance motor cyclists clearing the road when he travelled around, plus two or three following cars of bodyguards. But these days the police may have been anxious for his welfare too, for they were much more aggressive in their demands to get one off the road. One could end up in a ditch if there was insufficient time to find a better parking place. One could also be arrested if thought to be deliberately uncooperative.

CHAPTER TWENTY NINE

FAREWELL

In the old days of Mau Mau, Kiambu had been named "Pangaland" because of all the atrocities committed there. It was sadly returning to that kind of state with so many armed robberies, people being killed, and others living in fear. Our night watchmen at the entrance to Anmer Estate were attacked one night but they fought like brave Somalis do and drove off the intruders. Next morning one of them had a large plaster across his forehead but still wore his usual grin as we drove out of the gate on our way to work. Sometimes at night we would hear the sound of drums - an eerie haunting reverberation. There were rumours amongst the Africans of new oathing ceremonies being carried out. We never knew against whom or what. We were jumpy and when a new night watchman for our house insisted on trying all our doors and windows at 2am each morning we told him not to do that as he was frightening us to death.

Another night we all awoke to the most horrible grinding, groaning noise and I slowly realised that it was one of the huge fir trees behind the house falling. If it came our way it would go right through the house. It was too late to act, so I wrapped my arms round my head and settled in the blankets. Then came the most thunderous crash as it fell to the ground, but it did not hit the house. The African quarters were narrowly missed by a mere two or three feet. What a scare! Next day it was agreed that the rest of the fir trees would have to be lopped down because they were of great age. It rather spoilt the grounds, but safety came first.

The next thing to upset us was a car accident. Driving home from work one night we had reached the turn off from the main road which led out to our coffee estate. There I had to stop with my right winky light flashing as an Asian funeral procession was coming towards us. It was a long motorcade and we waited patiently. I occasionally checked the rear mirror but was not unduly worried as it was a wide road and I had left ample space for any car or even bus to get by. Then I noticed a white car come over the brow of the hill behind us. I was still unconcerned, but on looking a second time my heart almost stopped beating. It was coming straight into the back of us at an unbelievable speed. There was no time for any action. I didn't remember anything until I came to, still in the driver's seat, and saw that our car was broadside across the road at least 100 yards up the road and that we were between two funeral cars! An Asian gentleman was looking in.

"Thank goodness," he said. "Are you alright? My goodness I saw all that and it was nothing to do with you. You were doing everything legal. He must be a mad man. If you want a witness, here is my card. I must go now as I am in the funeral party."

Off he went; we struggled out. The boot was in the back seat. Wheels were buckled, tyres all flat, petrol and water had all run out on the road. We were dazed but thought we were all okay. We could see the white car way up on the left in the ditch. Elaine marched off to shout,

"Who is the driver of this car?" Then she saw him badly cut and she promptly collapsed on the grass verge. We all had to sit on the grass then as we suffered from shock. Hundreds of Africans very quickly surrounded us and then thankfully we saw two young European men stop their car and run over. They were schoolteachers from the Catholic school at Kiambu and they were really marvellous. Quickly they helped us to their car and drove us to Kiambu hospital. One of them ran in and a short while later walked out with a very dubious look on his face,

"Gosh, if you don't think you are dying, I wouldn't go in there," he said.

"Shall we go to Nairobi then?" asked the other one.

I intervened and said, "Please just take us home. We don't live far from here and I can then phone our doctor."

We had to pass by our wrecked car on the way back and found that the police had already arrived on the scene. An African inspector came over to ask if it was ours. I said yes and he told me that I must drive it off the road as it was obstructing the traffic. Looking at the car I didn't know how we were still alive. It looked like a distorted concertina.

"You must be joking!" I said. I could have cried.

It was a new Cortina, only 6 weeks in my possession. One of the young men told him the car could not possibly be driven in its present state and we arranged for the police pick-up truck to take it to Kiambu police station. The white car which was a taxi was still there, but the driver and passengers had disappeared. The inspector only told us that the brakes had failed. He needed a report from me but our rescuers said that I was too shocked and they were taking us to hospital.

We were soon home and the young men rang our doctor, gave us tea and aspirins and waited until the doctor arrived. They visited us later several times to make sure we recovered and became good friends. Luckily the doctor found no broken ribs or other bones. He thoroughly examined every inch of our bodies and then gave his verdict which was to stay in bed for 48 hours in case of any internal injury showing up. My goodness, next day we couldn't move, so sore and stiff and battered we felt. Elaine's legs were bruised black and blue up to the knees. After a week we were able to return to work. Even today I still watch everything behind me very carefully when I drive.

The end of the affair was that the taxi driver had no licence, no insurance, very little driving experience, so my own insurance had to pay for a new car. The police never called for a court case and within a month or two we saw the same driver shooting up and down the road in his repaired taxi!

After Independence it was the dream of every African to possess a car. High officials chose Mercedes. Inexperienced drivers, licence or no, turned the highways into death traps. They had no respect for rules of the road and there were many most dreadful accidents. We saw a lorry which had gone over the side of a bridge at the foot of a hill. Parts of the lorry had got caught up in the bridge construction and it was hanging straight down over the river. We heard later that it had been carrying about 30 Africans home from work and they had all been tossed out. The driver was killed, some were drowned, and others injured.

One morning on the way to work I saw a car following me down a hill at a crazy speed. The driver had no control so I pulled in very close to the side and he shot past. Now he had to climb a long rise at the top of which I knew was a bend in the road. We followed and witnessed the greatest 'stunt act' ever. At the top of the hill when he could not take the bend the car shot off to the left, air bound. There was a valley at the side of the road planted with large pine trees. The car continued to fly through the air missing every tree and landed on the opposite bank still upright! I had pulled up and I saw the driver open the door, step out and walk away. A lone cyclist, who joined me and had also seen the event said,

"Allah! Memsahib! Sawa sawa rocket!" (Just like a rocket!)

Maureen was again very ill. Tests showed that she had bilharzia, most probably from camping on the shores of a lake on a filming outing. We became deeply concerned. After treatment in Nairobi Hospital we thought she would never pick up, so thin and wan she looked. Medical care was very expensive and a prolonged illness could delve deeply into one's financial reserves. We talked again of leaving, but knew we must wait until she was stronger. We still did not wish to leave and tried to analyse why when so many dreadful things were happening. I concluded that Africa bewitches one, especially our Kenya which is so beautiful.

We found it hard to accept that our days in this beloved land were running out. The final decision had to come after Elaine and I, travelling home one evening as darkness was falling, became aware that a car was following us on the lonely road through the coffee. Across a valley, we realised another car on the bank was stationary and flicking its lights.

"Oh no!" we both breathed, "surely we're not trapped?"

Elaine was driving. The car ahead then moved on in the direction of our home, which lulled us into believing our imagination had been playing tricks. Maybe someone had just stopped, maybe the car behind was someone on their way home. We carried on down the valley, up the other side, over the crest and down a further valley. Then to our dismay, we saw that the car ahead had again stopped at the foot of the hill and was broadside across the road.

"What shall I do?" anxiously asked Elaine.

We could not see the car behind us yet; Elaine pulled up. The car ahead now proceeded to turn towards us, but on backing a little, it miraculously dropped into a marshy area on the left hand side of the road. They must have been strangers to the area as this was a deep marsh covered by reeds and bulrushes and definitely a place to avoid with a vehicle. We could now see the car turning over on its side. At this moment, the following car appeared over the brow of the hill.

"What shall I do?" again pleaded Elaine.

"Drive like the wind!" I shouted, "with luck we'll get by before they get out of the car."

She certainly put her foot down, and as we roared past, we saw at least six Africans struggling to disentangle themselves from the vehicle, which was settling further and further into the quagmire. Blessedly, we were only a half mile from home, which we reached safely, and where we knew no harm would befall us. We had been so lucky to escape. All evening, from our verandah, we could hear our prospective assailants struggling to retrieve their (possibly stolen) car.

That night we quietly talked of leaving, seriously. We knew that we had had many lucky escapes from personal harm, and I knew also, that I was not prepared to go on tempting providence as regards the safety of my beloved girls. This was no longer our Kenya of happy, carefree days when law and order was taken for granted.

And so, gradually over the weeks, we sorted out all the affairs our leaving entailed. Now and again we wept a little, now and then we worried about life in a new country, but we knew we had to go.

It was the biggest wrench of our lives to walk away from the country we loved, the country we had hoped would succeed in sheltering our society, in which we wished only to live, work and contribute as much as possible to that country's future prosperity. It was not to be, and there on a bleak, wet morning was the old sub-chief telling us that Kiambu was crying because we were leaving...!